With
Special Gree...
From
The Author

Chester E. Swor
Philippians 1:3 and 20, 21
Numbers 6: 24-26

Very truly
Yours _____

Very truly Yours

CHESTER E. SWOR

BROADMAN PRESS
Nashville, Tennessee

Printed in the United States of America
5AT54KSP

Foreword

So many of you have urged for long that some of my messages which had become your favorites be put into writing. Though I have wanted to accede to your generous and cordial request sooner, the heavy schedules and the limited writing time hitherto have made practically impossible my doing so. Several favorable circumstances have now coincided to make this book possible.

The title, *Very Truly Yours,* comes straight from my heart, for these messages are far more yours than mine. You gave to me the inspiration to prepare them for their original use in conferences, assemblies, and church meetings. You have given to me the vital personal experiences and life-size illustrations which walk through the messages. With your abiding interest and with your fervent prayers you have sustained my lay ministry of helping Christians to walk closer to Jesus.

The least I can do to requite your generosity toward me is to give back to you now in permanent form the messages which you have helped so largely to make. Here they are: the messages which you have asked for more frequently than any others which I have delivered in the morning watch services and the campfire meetings. You are so welcome to use them in any way which brings joy to you and strength to others. Please help yourself to them, for they are, as are the love and gratitude of their author,

VERY TRULY YOURS!

Acknowledgments

I T IS PROBABLY IMPOSSIBLE TO LIST AND thank all the people who help to make any book. Such is surely true of this one. So many have offered suggestions, inspiration, and encouragement. To these many friends, unnamed here but cherished in my heart, a debt of immense gratitude is felt.

It is possible, however, to thank specifically some who have facilitated the actual preparation of the messages for printing. Among the friends who have made possible the secretarial work involved are Dr. James Nelson, Rev. Luther Holcomb, Messrs. Edgar and Henry Harris, Mr. Frank Patterson, and Mr. Hudson Titmus. For the favor which these friends have accorded I am profoundly grateful.

The bulk of the mechanical preparation of the manuscripts has been done by Kenneth S. Jones. His work in taking the messages down by recorder and in turning them into manuscripts has been indispensable and is appreciated almost infinitely. In the final stages of preparation, superlatively valuable help was rendered by Mrs. R. P. Blake and Miss Mary Jean Aiken. To them goes my warm and earnest gratitude.

Though into the fabric of these twelve messages have been woven strands of information and inspiration given to me by many people in many places, I feel a particular debt of gratitude to Dr. Solon B. Cousins of the University of Richmond in connection with the message which is entitled "The Taste Test." In a cherished period of conversation years ago, Dr. Cousins shared with me some thinking on Job 6:6 which added greatly to my own ideas. To Dr. Cousins and to others whose specific contributions may be unconsciously reflected here, I am warmly, vastly grateful.

CHESTER E. SWOR

Contents

One

The Shadow Test

"And believers were the more added to the Lord, multitudes both of men and women. Insomuch that they brought forth the sick into the streets, and laid them on beds and couches, that at the least the shadow of Peter passing by might overshadow some of them." Acts 5:14–15.

NOW THAT CHRIST HAD GONE BACK TO HIS Father in heaven, Peter had assumed somewhat the leadership of the believers in Jerusalem. He was speaking with such spiritual power and logic that he was invincible. He was healing with such unmistakable power from God that the miracles were doubtless the talk of the city. Because medicine and surgery as we understand them today were practically non-existent as professions then, these acts of healing were particularly welcome and thrilling. Evidently the confidence of the people in his power to heal must have grown rapidly and profoundly as the instances of healing multiplied.

Of course, there were many people who could not get their sick ones down to central places where much of the preaching and healing occurred. Too, there were no "stated hours" for Peter's appearances. Therefore, in Acts 5:14–15 there is the inspiring picture of devoted people who were putting their sick ones on beds

and couches in the streets, probably outside the door-
ways of their homes, hoping with a prayer that Peter
would come up or down that street that day—"that at
the least the shadow of Peter passing by might overshadow some of them."

People in the city of Jerusalem had such profound
confidence in the power which they had seen in the life
of Peter that they believed that even his physical
shadow, falling across sick ones on beds and couches
along the street down which Peter walked, would perform a cure. Never a finer compliment was paid to anybody's Christianity than that!

Two preliminary observations are in order. First,
these people would have had no more confidence in
Peter's shadow than they had in the shadow of a tree if
they had not discovered a power in his life which was
not found in the life of the average person. They were
not putting their sick ones out to be touched by just
anybody's shadow. They were putting them there to be
touched by Peter's shadow.

Second, Peter's life would not have had this confi-
dence-inspiring power had he not met and followed
Jesus and had he not permitted Jesus to control his life
completely. The closeness to Jesus with which he
walked brought the power; the power in his life
brought the confidence in his shadow.

We cast shadows, too, spiritual shadows called influence. And, as in Peter's instance, the effectiveness of
our shadows will depend upon whether or not we have
met and followed Jesus and upon the degree to which

4

we permit him to control our lives. In the light of your nearness to Jesus, therefore, what sort of shadow are you casting into the lives of the people who are touched by it in your journey up and down the street of every-day living?

Our English word "influence" is a beautiful and descriptive word. It comes directly from a Latin participle which means "flowing into." Therefore, it describes a continuing process in which there is a very real flow of power-through-example from one person to another. If it were possible for us to distinguish everything in our lives which came to us through the influences of other people—both those who have touched our lives directly and those who have touched us through the written word, most of us would find that we are an amazing composite of other people's influences. In the same logic, other people are being made up, in part, from the influences which flow from us to them through the power of example.

One's influence does not cease when death comes; it continues to walk the earth to touch other people's lives. To this hour, the influence of Christopher Wren is felt vitally in architectural circles around the world. Florence Nightingale's influence is seen in every school of nursing in our Christian society. The influence of Thomas Edison is present in almost every room of our homes. The influence of Jesus Christ, over 1900 years after his ascension, is the most powerful single dynamic in the daily living of millions of people.

Whether or not we know it or wish it, we are casting

shadows, some of which may help to determine the destiny of someone else. While every one of us ponders the important impact of his own shadow, three challenging truths need to be mentioned.

I

God can use our shadows as a medium through which he can work to touch and transform the lives of other people. There is a widespread, but erroneous feeling among great numbers of Christians to the effect that it is not possible for them to wield large influence because they cannot speak effectively in public delivery, nor teach convincingly, nor sing inspiringly, nor participate otherwise in the normally accepted modes of leadership. The Christian who comes to that conclusion is failing to remember that, in the final analysis, the acceptability of the messages and performances of gifted religious leaders depends largely upon the *quality of Christian living* which those persons have demonstrated prior to making leadership appearances. Men will dismiss the most eloquent religious talk with contemptuous scorn if they know that the personal living of the speaker does not measure up to Christian principle.

Therefore, regardless of the fact that you may not be able to compete in the limelight, you can do the main thing: You can live the kind of life that casts the kind of shadow through which God can work to touch other people's lives. The greatest need of Christianity in America today is not for more eloquent speaking in its

6

behalf, but for more consistent living of its principles in shops and stores, in businesses and professions, in sororities and fraternities, at home and abroad, everywhere!

In a youth meeting in which I was speaking, a young man of distinguished appearance from a nearby campus came forward one evening to confess faith in Christ. His coming affected his fellow students perceptibly; therefore, I knew that his decision represented a tremendous victory. After the service, he indicated an urgent desire to chat with me. An appointment was made for him to join me the next evening. In the course of our conversation, I asked him to point out the most influential factor in his decision to become a Christian. Knowing that my message on the night before had been a message directed almost exclusively to Christians, I sensed that some other factor had brought him. He told an inspiring story.

He had been in the Marine Corps and had come out of service most thoroughly hardened in many ways. He was cynical and sarcastic to degrees which won for him the reputation of being an agnostic. Because his father had insisted, he had entered this Christian college. From the day of his appearance on the college campus he delighted to shock fellow students with his lack of religious belief, actually insulting some of the ministerial students who sought to win him to faith in Christ. He laughed raucously when people invited him to devotional meetings. He ridiculed the entire program of religious life on the campus.

7

But he could not resist the influence of the perfectly wonderful Christian girl who sat next to him in history class. Though he had been able to resist the appeals, approaches, and arguments of the students who had sought him, he could not resist the unanswerable argument of Christianity as presented in the goodness, tenderness, gentleness, sweetness, radiance, and power of a girl who lived so close to Jesus that only the word "consecration" could adequately describe her life.

A vacant period following history class made it possible for the ex-Marine to escort the lovely Christian girl to her dormitory or to a nearby drugstore for refreshment each day. Eventually he asked for an explanation of the wonderful differences in her life which had impressed him so deeply. She was a demure person, not at all given to speech-making. Therefore, she replied simply, "Really, I am not conscious that there is anything unusual in my life; but if there is something which has impressed you, it has come because of my relationship to Jesus. I am trying to be the best Christian possible."

That reply was more eloquent than speeches, books, and arguments. The young man recognized immediately that the only explanation of the attractiveness of the life which had so won his admiration was that she had met Christ and that she was following him faithfully—the Christ whom he had so vigorously resisted. The student concluded his explanation in these words: "My coming to Jesus was the result of the irresistible presentation of Christianity in the daily living of a sophomore girl."

On another campus I heard much of a magnificent young woman whose influence had touched all the campus and her own dormitory particularly. She was not striking in beauty, she was not involved in campus politics, she was not a sorority member; yet, she was so consistent and winsome in her daily Christian living that when she walked up or down the halls of her dormitory, her dormitory mates often confessed to each other, "She is the sort of person we all ought to be." She never made a public speech, she was never on the platform or in the limelight, she never composed a poem nor wrote a book nor sang a solo; but she lived so close to Jesus that every little influence which emanated from her life was the sort of shadow which lifted and strengthened someone else.

In a church to which I had gone for a youth week, a leading layman and his wife were youth counselors. I sensed immediately that they were of tremendous influence in the young life of the church and community. They were radiant and dynamic Christians. It was my assumption that they had been Christians for many years. Therefore, I was both surprised and thrilled to learn in a later conversation with them that they had been won to Christ through the power of the example of their young son. He had found his way to church and to Christ without the attendance of his parents and despite their miserable example.

The inspiration of this story is this: the lad had never made a speech to his parents. He had simply met Jesus and had walked with him in such day-after-day

9

faithfulness that the radiance of his shadow was used of God to touch and transform his mother and dad. The right kind of shadow will convey transforming power!

II

Sometimes a person, touched and transformed through your shadow or mine, is so gifted that *he may be used of God to touch thousands of people*. The thrill of this possibility is that the Christian who casts the first shadow will have the joy of knowing that his shadow is touching indirectly every one of those thousands; and, in my judgment, God will not forget that this gifted person would not be casting helpful shadows at all, had not your shadow or mine first touched him. We who are less talented than others may not achieve immortality of reputation on the basis of our accomplishments, but we can achieve immortality of influence by living the kind of life that casts the kind of shadow through which God can work.

Behind the life of the great Japanese Christian, Kagawa, is the shadow of a dedicated missionary. Behind the life of the missionary is the shadow of a devout Sunday school teacher who was God's instrument in touching the lad who later went into foreign missions. Behind the people who have blessed the world most through Christian witness, almost invariably there stand the shadows of humble, often unknown persons whose influence was God's medium of contact. Even though the world may not know or may not remember these unheralded people, God never forgets them or fails to accord to them a part of the credit for the accomplishments of the "greater lights."

III

There are times in which we cast our most important shadows when we are *not even conscious that we are influencing people at all*. When we are farthest away from the church, in the midst of circumstances which we do not think to be propitious, we may be nearest to someone who needs a tug toward Christ. In buses, in crowded stores, in bustling corridors, in classrooms, on vacation jaunts, or in an endless number of other situations which would never be thought of as "influence opportunities," there may be someone standing by, looking on, listening in with a hungry heart. There is no time in which our shadows are not potential!

Years ago there came to our campus a student whose parents had sent him there "to be influenced." He, knowing of their purpose and being out of harmony with it, had resolved not to be influenced by the Christian purposes of the college. He almost succeeded in his resolution! Though he sat in my Sunday school class, he was adamant to all of my attempts to impress him with the application of Christian truth to daily behavior. Though I directed several chapel talks toward his problems, I would have made as discernible an impression in addressing Gibraltar, because he knew that I was trying to influence him. In short, when I had my "influencing clothes" on, I made no progress with him.

Near the end of the session, he was one of several

students riding with me in a newly purchased car of which I was extremely proud and of which I had asked the students to help me take excellent care. We were driving into a nearby city to perform a small pre-supper chore. As we approached a very busy intersection, the driver of the car behind mine was fascinated by a wedding party which was descending the steps of a nearby church. Failing to notice that the traffic in front of him had stopped, he drove full speed into the rear of my cherished new car. I was sick at heart in the quick realization that serious damage had been done.

The crowd gathered quickly as the traffic officer arrived to supervise the scene. Feeling that if there is a time in which a negligent driver should be severely lectured, that time is not in the presence of a crowd, I chatted with the driver in Christian spirit, accepting his explanation, assuring him that upon his assumption of the financial responsibility there were no feelings of unkindness in my heart toward him. He was grateful for my attitude; he apologized again and invited me to his home for dinner in the future. I thanked him, he thanked me, and we parted in fine spirit.

That night, as I sat at the desk in my dormitory office, the student who had vowed not to be influenced in this Christian college, slipped quietly in, stood at my desk, and said with earnest feeling: "I just want to tell you that the way you behaved in the accident this afternoon was the finest demonstration of Christian spirit I have seen, and I couldn't go to bed without coming by to tell you that you have influenced me very deeply."

As the student turned to walk out of my office, I sat almost stunned by the realization that in an automobile accident eight miles from the campus at 5:30 in the afternoon, I had had my first real opportunity to influence that student. That experience brought to me, in never-to-be-forgotten manner, the challenging and almost terrifying reminder that we often cast our most significant shadows when we are not even conscious that we are influencing people at all. It brought to me then, as I hope it brings to your heart now, the resolution to try valiantly to live the Christian spirit comprehensively, so that every shadow cast will be one which God can use.

What is your shadow doing to other people?

Dear Father, while we thank thee with all our hearts for the blessed shadows of people who have helped to make us what we are, we pray fervently that thou wilt help us to remember constantly that our shadows are helping to make or break other people. May our shadows ever help, never hurt those whom they touch. Amen.

Two

The Taste Test

"Can that which is unsavoury be eaten without salt? Or is there any taste in the white of an egg?" Job 6:6.

HAVE YOU EVER HAD THE EXPERIENCE of running across a quaint Old Testament verse, thinking for a moment that you had never seen it before? Such a feeling was mine when I "discovered" Job 6:6. Though I must have seen it in my times of reading the Bible all through, I had on this occasion the zestful pleasure of a first-time sampling.

If we were in an English classroom, we would classify that quaint verse as a double rhetorical question: a question asked *not* in the expectation that the hearer or reader will answer audibly, but for the purpose of provoking thought. In that spirit, let us look again into the two questions asked in this quaint verse.

"Can that which is unsavoury be eaten without salt?" Your mind responds immediately with the observation that there are some dishes of food which would not be palatable and which you would not like if the salt were omitted. The average dish of vegetables, for instance, would taste flat, if not insipid, if the salt were left out.

Internationally famous Dixie corn bread would be no longer popular with the Southern palate if there were no salt in it. Other favorite dishes would suffer a similar loss of their flavorful appeal in the absence of salt. Though the amount of salt put into the dish of food is almost microscopic when compared with the total weight of the food, that significant bit of salt makes a determining difference in taste and acceptability for most people.

"Is there any taste in the white of an egg?" Have you eaten the uncooked, "undoctored" white of an egg? If so, you will remember that it is almost flavorless. Though millions of Americans take eggs at breakfast, very few of them fail to add a dash of salt or a dash of pepper. Again, the amount of salt added to the food is negligible in weight, but it makes a palatable difference in the taste of the egg.

So much for the rhetorical questions; now what thinking do they provoke? Though every reader or hearer may well be led into a different trend of thought, the thought which the questions of that verse provoked in my heart is this: just as to the dish of food or to the egg a dash of salt needs to be added for zest and flavor, so *to the Christian's profession of Christianity there must be added the practice of Christian living* if his Christianity is to "taste good" to the people who sample it in daily contact. A pervasive demonstration of Christian spirit and a practical living of Christian teaching will make the individual's life so flavorful that those who sample it in daily relationships will like the

18

taste, will want more of it, and some will want to know the recipe!

How does *your* Christianity taste to the people who sample it? Are there grimaces of face which say unmistakably, "I want no more of that"? Or are there quiet smiles of gratification which say just as unmistakably, "I like the taste of your Christianity so much that I want to be more often with you; in fact, I want the recipe for your life"?

On the assumption that all of us sincerely want our Christianity to pass the taste test, I am pointing out four requisites to flavorful, attractive Christian living.

I

We must have a genuine experience with Christ: an experience no less than regeneration. The person who has not been born again will not only experience a lack of joy and victory in his attempt to live Christ's teaching, but he will, also, present to the sampling world a life which has the surface of Christianity but not the soul of it, the appearance of Christianity but not the taste of it. The surest, quickest, complete basis for disgust on the part of those who sample our lives in daily contact is their suspecting or discovering that you and I are not genuinely Christian. Hypocrisy is to be despised in any area of life, but it is doubly unfortunate in the area of one's relationship to Jesus.

In sensing our genuineness or lack of it in the matter of belonging to Jesus, many people need only limited contact with us. Some of them sense instinctively from a single touch with us that we carry on the pretense of Christianity without possessing the power of salvation. Though our labels had marked us as Christians, the sampling of our lives had proved that we were not.

In one of my rare invasions of grocery stores I ran across some little bottles of liquid in brilliant colors of orange, lime, grape, and strawberry. The labels declared that if the contents were put into the proper amount of water and sufficiently sweetened, the result would be a refreshing drink tasting exactly like orangeade and other such drinks. In view of the fact that the cost per bottle was extremely low, I concluded that here was a real bargain. To make sure that there would be adequate quantity to last through the very warm weather which was then in effect, I purchased a half dozen of the bottles.

My mother, wiser in grocery purchasing than I, was not enthusiastic for my investment but obligingly prepared the orange drink according to the label's directions. In the glass pitcher the drink looked like genuine orangeade and, had I not tasted it, I could have been deceived into believing it to be genuine. In keen anticipation, I poured a glass full of the promising ade, sipped it, and discovered instantaneously that it was entirely synthetic, with little resemblance to genuine orange. I had the sensation that I was drinking diluted turpentine with a faint artificial orange flavor! The drink looked genuine in both bottle and pitcher, but when submitted to the taste test, it failed miserably.

There are many Christians in our day who perform

eloquently and effectively in a variety of church activities and who, when viewed from the pews, look and sound like genuine followers of Jesus; but who, when submitted to revealing pressures, are discovered to be devoid of the indispensable experience with Jesus called regeneration. The Christian who can join Paul in saying, "I know whom I have believed," has the first prerequisite for passing the taste test.

II

There must be the flavor of the personal note in our Christian witness. You can probably name immediately some Christians the genuineness of whose salvation you do not doubt, but from whom you have almost never heard the ring of a fresh, vital, personal testimony. When they speak of prayer in terms of its power to change things, they cannot point out actual experiences in their own lives. When they speak of victories through faith, they are obliged to quote the experiences of other Christians. When they extol Christ for his adequacy in meeting our needs, they are not able to document with personal experiences.

There is something in the freshness and flavor of the personal note in Christianity for which there is no substitute. When the Christian can say, "I *know* that surrender brings dividends, I *know* that it pays to serve Jesus, I *know* that soul winning brings an incomparable joy," he is putting vitality and flavor into the taste of his Christianity.

Once I was registering for a term of graduate study.

As was the custom, we were registering in the gymnasium of the university. From walls and balcony rails many advertisements of eating places were suspended. All of those placards were of the dull, mechanical sort with nothing of personal appeal. Had one wanted to be dramatic, he could have asked one of the placards, "How do you know that the eating place which you advertise is a good one? Have you eaten there?" Had the placard been endowed with speech, it would have been obliged to reply, "To tell the truth, I have never eaten there. I am simply repeating another's opinion."

In the midst of the morning there ambled into the gymnasium a tremendous young man of far more than two hundred pounds of weight. He was wearing placards which announced to the throng of registrants, "EAT AT MRS. ARCHER'S. I DID!" Everybody who saw the advertisement agreed that its personal note was magnificent. The boy's very appearance seemed to declare: "When I came to the university, I was pale and wan; but see what Mrs. Archer's cooking did!"

An interesting footnote is that Mrs. Archer's had more diners that term than ever before. There is no substitute for the personal note in any kind of testimony. Particularly is there no substitute for the personal note in the testimony of a Christian if he wants his Christianity to pass the taste test.

III

In the third place, if our Christianity is to taste good to the people who sample it, it must be permitted to make us increasingly attractive. Regardless of the natural asset or handicap of one's physical appearance, he or she will become more beautiful in spirit as the spirit of Christ increasingly controls the heart. The Christ-controlled heart diffuses a radiant attractiveness through every facet of personality.

There ought to be something in the eyes of a Christian that suggests gentleness, love, sympathy, understanding, patience, forgiveness, and compassion in the heart. There ought to be something in the face of a Christian that suggests, "There is a peace in my heart that passes understanding." There ought to be something in the voice of a Christian that indicates friendship and unselfishness. There ought to be something in the total atmosphere of a Christian's life that is as fragrant as perfume, indicating to all whom he touches, "Jesus possesses my heart completely." That kind of Christian will be attractive. That kind of Christianity will pass the taste test.

In one of our colleges there were two dietitians in quick succession. Insofar as the menus were concerned, they served almost exactly the same foods. The first dietitian, though an excellent person, had no concept of attractiveness in the serving of foods. Spinach was heaped on large platters and had to be disentangled before it could be eaten; sliced pineapple was poured into large bowls and had to be "speared" as the bowls passed around the table; other foods were cooked and served in a dull, colorless fashion.

The second dietitian served the same foods but

23

served them so much more attractively. She, too, felt that college students needed spinach, but she knew the attitude of the average student toward that food. Therefore, she had the spinach served in individual servers with chips of hard-boiled egg atop each serving. More spinach was consumed than ever before, and the compliments concerning its good taste were bountiful. Though she served the same grade of sliced pineapple, she served it as a salad with grated cheese atop it. The students were almost unanimous in declaring that the food was so much better than that served by the preceding regime. As a matter of fact, the food itself was no better; yet, the more attractive serving had made the food immeasurably more palatable and attractive!

There are two Christians, both genuinely saved. One Christian is cold, critical, selfish, "holier than thou" in attitude. The second Christian is warm, winsome, humble, unassuming, gentle, kind, and gracious in attitude. It is unnecessary to ask, "Which of these Christians is the more attractive? Which type of Christianity will better pass the sampling world's taste test?" Though there is no difference in the salvation of these two Christians, there is tremendous difference in the presentation of their Christianity to the world!

IV

We must live our Christianity comprehensively if we wish it to pass the taste test. This means that the student must live his Christianity just as consistently in the classroom, in the laboratory, in the dormitory, on the football field, in his dating, as he lives it on Sundays. This means that the business and professional worker must practice without compromise the teachings of Christ for our personal living. This means that the Christian will live his Christianity just as radiantly in the privacy of his home as he does when he is in the limelight of religious performance. This means that all of us who are Christians will be as thoroughly Christian in our social and recreational activities as we profess to be in times of religious testimony. If people discover lapses in your Christianity and mine, areas in which we do not practice what we profess to believe, they will develop a vehement distaste for our presentation of Christianity.

I visited a church many years ago in which there was a layman who was much in demand as a speaker. He was unusually dynamic on the platform. When his wife invited me to be one of several luncheon guests in their home, I went with keen anticipation, feeling sure that a close-up contact with this Christian layman would be inspiring. My disappointment was terrific!

He had evidently not been advised of the coming of the visitors and was, therefore, displeased. He was unkind to his wife, unsympathetic toward his children, and uncouth in his table manners. He raced through his meal and then read the newspaper in the faces of invited guests. The formulators of table etiquette would have been profoundly abashed! The Christ whose name he bore must have been grieved that he had failed to live his Christianity comprehensively.

25

The visitors in his household wished no further taste of his Christianity!

To conclude in happier vein: I visit a professional man's office frequently, always coming away with a glow of happiness. This man lives his Christianity comprehensively. His closest associates believe him to be the best Christian in the city; his wife and children know him to be a genuine Christian in the tensest moments of home stress; his neighbors cannot recall an instance in which he has not displayed the Christian spirit.

Two college boys said to me: "Wish you could know our Dad. He is the finest Christian we know. You couldn't grow up around him without wanting to be a Christian." A businessman said of a young woman employee: "I have seen her in every irritating circumstance imaginable in this business, but she is always a Christian." Christianity comprehensively lived tastes good!

How does your Christianity taste to the people who sample it?

Heavenly Father, send every one of us away from this meditation with the high resolution of heart to know Christ genuinely, to experience his guidance and promises personally, to portray his spirit attractively, to live his teachings comprehensively, that people may taste and know that the Lord is good. Amen.

Three

The Fruit Test

"*And he left them, and went out of the city into Bethany; and he lodged there. Now in the morning when he returned into the city, he hungered. And when he saw a fig tree in the way, he came to it, and found nothing thereon, but leaves only, and said unto it, Let no fruit grow on thee henceforward for ever. And presently the fig tree withered away.*" Matthew 21:17–19.

WHY SHOULD A FRUIT TREE HAVE TAKEN away from it the chance of continued existence? A short and sure answer is this: *a fruit tree which does not produce fruit does not honestly deserve to live.* Though it may have a substantial trunk, well-developed limbs, copious and attractive leaves and blossoms, a fruit tree has failed in the prime purpose for its existence if it does not in time and in season produce its fruit.

Luke 13:6–9 presents in brief, but unmistakable, clarity the attitude of Jesus toward fruitless fruit trees. After looking in vain for three years for fruit from a fig tree in his vineyard, the owner ordered his vine dresser to cut the tree down. "Why cumbereth it the ground?" was the owner's affirmation stated in question form. The reply of the vine dresser is indicative of both long-suffering patience and eventual justice: "Lord, let it alone this year also, till I shall dig about it and dung it: and if it bear fruit, well: and if not, then after that thou shalt cut it down."

You and I are, in a very real way, trees growing in God's vineyard of grace and opportunity. We have been surrounded by many magnificent opportunities for cultivating spiritual strength. Many of us, like fruit trees, have been drinking in liberally of these God-provided blessings: we have read his Word, we have exercised the privilege of prayer, we have partaken freely of the spiritual food made possible in the well-balanced church program. In short, we have basked in his love, feasted on his goodness, luxuriated in his mercy.

If fruit trees, having drunk liberally of God's provisions for them, do not deserve to live in perpetual fruitlessness, you and I most surely are no more worthy of our places in God's vineyard if we are not transmuting some of the spiritual strength of our lives into spiritual fruit. Fruit trees and Christians do not deserve to live if they do not bear fruit!

Though *witnessing* and *serving* are not the only fruits which a Christian's life ought to produce, they are two principal ones: witnessing so effectively that soul-winning ensues, serving so fully that every talent is used. As this study proceeds, each one of us can profitably ask himself, "In the light of the Christian witnessing and serving to which I have given myself up to now, do I honestly deserve to live?"

I

In the Christian's life fruit bearing is not an elective course; it is a required course. It is not required for salvation, thank God, for our salvation is by grace and not by works "lest any man should boast." But fruit bearing is imperative in the Christian's life if that life is to mean its maximum to him, to those who observe his life, and to the progress of the kingdom of heaven.

Fruit bearing is necessary for *growth*. There is no such person as a growing Christian who is not also a fruit-bearing Christian. Fruit bearing is necessary for *joy*. Christians who are busy in witnessing and serving are Christians whose lives are characterized by spiritual happiness. Fruit bearing is necessary for *maximum usefulness*, for God will not bring increasing opportunity to a Christian who is not fully using his present capacities. Fruit bearing is necessary if the Christian's life is to be of *maximum inspiration* to others. Everybody reacts with a thrill to a fruit tree bountifully laden with wonderful fruit. Fruit bearing is imperative to *good stewardship of life*, for God's "Well done, thou good and faithful servant" will not come to those who have not been fully faithful with the capacities entrusted to them.

II

In the Christian's life fruit bearing is expected in proportion to the talents with which that life is endowed and in proportion to the opportunities for witnessing and serving with which that person is surrounded.

Suppose that the fig tree from which Jesus took away the privilege of continued existence had had the ability to talk and that it had remonstrated thus with Jesus:

"Lord, it is not fair that you should take away from me the opportunity for continued existence on the basis of my having no fruit. You see, Lord, I looked about me at the beautiful peaches and pears and plums on other fruit trees and decided to try my hand at those fruits. First, I tried to produce peaches, but no success came. Then I tried valiantly to produce a few pears, but not a one appeared. Finally I decided that, though plums are not as glamorous, I would try to produce plums. But you see, Lord, there is not a plum on my branches. I surely wanted to produce fruit. I tried, but there just wasn't anything I could do."

Silly? No more so than many, many Christians who say almost the same thing: "Why, there isn't any service I can render. I could not possibly teach a Sunday school class, nor even preside over it. I cannot possibly sing, and I am sure that I would quake with ghastly fear if I were called upon to do anything on the platform. I can't conduct a Bible drill. I can't direct socials. I can't preside in a circle. I just simply do not have the capacity to witness and serve!"

To both the fig tree and the Christian described here, Christ would be justified in saying, "He who created you knows your capacities perfectly; and, while not expecting you to do the things which you cannot do, he does expect you to bear the fruit, however small, for which you have the capacity." While not expecting the fig tree to produce peaches, pears, and plums, he did expect it to bear figs. If all the fig tree could honestly produce had been one tiny fig, Christ would surely have smiled a commendation of "Well done" upon it. While not expecting Christians to teach or preside or sing or conduct or lead if they honestly cannot do those things, he does expect all of us to do what we can do in witnessing and serving. *There is no Christian in God's vineyard who cannot produce some fruit, small though it be.*

He stands in the presence of your life and mine right now, knowing the capacities and opportunities with which we are endowed, looking so earnestly for fruit in proportion to these endowments. Does he turn away with sorrow that there is no fruit there? Does he turn away with regret that there is not fruit there in proportion to our fruit-bearing capacities?

III

In the light of Christ's expectation that we produce fruit in proportion to our capacities and opportunities, there are three groups of Christians who need special reminders.

First, there is a reminder to the many-talented Christian that he is expected to use every one of his talents in fruit bearing. The parable of the talents (Matt. 25) is most conclusive on this point! Suppose that the man with five talents had reasoned that he could use two of his talents and be doing as much as anybody else in his group. In that instance he would have been only a forty percenter in God's sight, for he would have been using only two out of his five talents.

"Or," the five-talented man might have rationalized,

"I shall use three of my talents and thereby be doing *more* than anybody else in my church." Though quantitatively he may have been doing more than anyone else among the people of whom he was a part, he would still have been only a sixty percenter, using only three of his five talents for the Lord who gave them. The many-talented Christian needs to compare his service life with what God gave him to use and not with the amount of service being rendered by others. Nothing short of fruit bearing to the maximum of one's ability is worthy!

Often I have had the genuine thrill of meeting a multi-talented Christian who, despite tremendous obligations in his business or profession, is using every God-given capacity in his church life. I remember a brilliant doctor who is highly successful in gynecology and obstetrics. At the time in which I visited his church, he was chairman of the deacons, he was teaching a Bible class, he sang in the choir, and he joined his pastor in soul-winning visits two nights each week. He was not only an excellent illustration of "all on the altar" in talents; he was, also, an eloquent refutation of the "I just don't have time" plaint of the great concourse of gifted people who are using only a pittance of their talents in witnessing and serving!

The second reminder is directed toward the person who feels that he is excused from serving, because he has handicaps which prevent his serving in the usual, conventional channels. There is the person who is severely handicapped by physical infirmity or deformity.

There is also the person whose life has been greatly hurt or distorted in other ways, so that the fruit bearing which he would have done normally is now impossible.

To the great throng of Christians who honestly cannot do the things in witnessing and serving which they would have done had not these handicaps come, there is this glorious truth: Those handicaps do not close the door to fruit bearing; instead, they simply open doors to other kinds of fruit bearing which, in the final analysis, may be more significant.

I remember with abiding inspiration a bedridden woman who had formerly taught the largest Sunday school class in her church, had sung in the choir, and had been most active in woman's work throughout the area. Her physical infirmity could not be cured; she would never be able to leave her bed until death came. She could never again witness and serve in the ways which had been dearest to her heart and truest to her abilities.

There were two possible attitudes from which she could choose. She could complain to the point of bitterness at the circumstances which robbed her of the opportunity for fruit bearing in the usual channels and, in a sense of utter frustration, decide that "My days are over. There's nothing else I can do." Or, in a spirit of consecrated courage she could say, "Though I cannot serve in the ways in which I want most to serve, I shall seek new ways; for handicaps so often do open new doors to service." I am delighted to report that this fine woman chose the latter course and became the most powerful witness in her little city.

During a week in which I spoke in her church, she called one hundred and fifty people over the telephone at her bedside, urging them to attend the meetings and sharing with them the reports of fine decisions being made. She invited many young people to sit at her bedside. Seven of these she led to faith in Christ; five others she led to the dedication of their lives to full-time Christian service. She made the greatest contribution to the special services; yet, she never left her bed. Her handicap had become an asset in fruit bearing!

In another city I visited a lovely woman who for nineteen years had been confined to a wheel chair, "promoted" there by a near-fatal automobile accident. Upon realizing that she could never walk again and that her life of Christian witness and service would have to be completely revised, she devoted herself to studying God's Word. She enlisted the help of some gifted Christians, availed herself of much help from commentaries and similar books, and with the indispensable aid of the Holy Spirit she came to an understanding of the Bible which brought total victory to her.

A wonderful by-product of this study, which was begun originally for her own strength, was her discovery that so many other people were searching for solutions to problems which only God's Word provides. Her present ministry of individual counseling and group Bible study has blessed the entire city. She now thanks God warmly for the handicap which, far from frustrating her desire to serve, has actually provided a throne of power from which to serve.

There is *no* handicap which cannot be turned into a medium of fruit bearing if the Christian wants with all his heart to bear fruit and if he dedicates the handicap with the prayer that God will use even that limitation to his glory. So, take another look at your physical handicap, or your difficult family background, or your lack of *anything* which you have mistakenly thought to be imperative to significant fruit bearing. Looked at through the eyes of the world, the ignominious cross was regarded to be a sure and fatal stigma to the name and message of Christ. Looked at through the eyes of God, that same cross became the medium through which the incomparable fruit of salvation was provided for a lost world. Look at your handicap this time through the eyes of God!

The third reminder is this: Let the little-talented Christian not conclude that because his talents are so few or so tiny, little difference will be made if he uses them or if he does not, and that, therefore, it doesn't matter whether he serves or not, or that what he can do does not matter in the progress of Christianity.

There is no Christian so limited in ability that there is not something he can do. Even if the thing is so ordinary, so commonplace, so removed from the public eye that it seems negligible, it matters to God that every Christian use even the "crumbs" of talent in fruit bearing.

37

Perhaps you can't teach that class, but you can *be there* with such fidelity that your very presence is an inspiration to the teacher. Perhaps you can't preach or sing, but you can certainly *pray* for the people who are preaching and singing, thereby adding power to their messages of word or song. Perhaps you can't preside or lead in your Sunday school class, but you can *invite* others with such radiance and persistence that they will begin to attend and, perhaps, experience a life transformation. It may well be that you can't serve in capacities which are essentially "limelight" positions; yet, you can *smile* with the love of God and the compassion of Jesus behind those smiles, melting barriers which more gifted Christians may not penetrate.

In his earthly ministry Jesus used so many "little" people and things in teaching his most memorable principles, in performing his most notable miracles, and in developing some of the most inspiring leadership for Christianity. We remember that Peter and John were alluded to in Acts 4:13 as "ignorant and unlearned"; yet, Peter, using all of his talent and empowered of the Holy Spirit, delivered the message at Pentecost, in response to which thousands of people became Christians. Jesus used a simple lad and a negligible lunch of loaves and fishes to perform a miracle in which the food-needs of five thousand persons were met. As materials with which to teach the magnificent lesson in humility, Jesus had no more than a common basin and a foot-towel. It is not so much what talent a person has to offer to Jesus that determines what

Jesus can do through him, but, rather, whether or not the individual is willing to permit Jesus to have every "loaf and fish" of his limited life.

Wiley was neither talented nor well educated. In fact, he had insuperable limitations which made impossible his doing a job higher in the world's scale of importance than selling daily newspapers on a downtown street intersection. He had two tiny talents, but he used them to their limit: He was optimistic perpetually, and he was faithful to the ultimate.

His optimism, based in his implicit faith in God, was so complete that nothing ever depressed him. His simple, but inspiring optimism crept through his calls as he announced his newspaper to the passing crowds. He never announced bad news except with a hopeful turn; he would announce tomorrow's weather forecast as "bright and sunny" while the rain poured down upon today! Business and professional men up and down that street will never forget Wiley's constant question when they gave evidence of depression: "What's wrong, Mister? God ain't dead yet, is he?"

Wiley's faithfulness inspired the circulation manager to perpetual eulogy. That same faithfulness to his church inspired teachers, preachers, and members. He couldn't do a thing in the program of his church except to attend, pray, listen, invite others, and pass out slips in the Sunday school class. Yet, the faithfulness with which he did those bits of service touched the hearts of many more talented members with reproof and inspiration.

39

When Wiley died, a whole city grieved his passing. Many of the most notable figures of the city and state attended his funeral; hundreds sent flowers; and all felt the common sentiment, "If all Christians were doing as nearly all they could do as Wiley did, this would be a wonderful world, indeed!" Many of us felt that when Wiley went into God's presence, he must surely have heard the coveted citation, "Well done, thou good and faithful servant."

To return to the frank, personal question of this message: Do I honestly deserve to live, or, like the barren fig tree, do I deserve because of my fruitlessness to lose the opportunity of continued living in God's garden? Many of us, doubtless, need to pray in the spirit of the prayer of the husbandman in Luke 13:6–9: "Lord, give me one more year!"

O merciful and long-suffering Father, we thank thee for thy patience in waiting so long for some of us to begin to bear fruit and to bear it in proportion to our capacities. We promise thee now that we shall try more faithfully to deserve these places in thy vineyard. Amen.

Four

The Touch Test

"*And, behold, a woman, which was diseased with an issue of blood twelve years, came behind him, and touched the hem of his garment: For she said within herself, If I may but touch his garment, I shall be whole.*" Matthew 9:20–21.

JESUS WAS SURROUNDED BY A GREAT crowd of people who were pressing very close to him. In the crowd there was a woman whose body was very badly impaired by an ailment called "an issue of blood." For years she had sought cures to no avail. Though medicine, as we understand it today, was barely in its kindergarten days, she had evidently gone the rounds and had exhausted the possibilities of a cure through normal channels.

As this distressed woman with the hope of a cure still burning in her heart pressed through the crowd, she was increasingly possessed of the conviction that Christ could and would heal her body. Evidently she felt that she was not important enough to stand in his presence, engage him in conversation, and consume his precious time. We see in her face the growing and glowing conviction of her heart: "If I may but touch his garment, I shall be made whole." Impelled by that conviction, she crept through the dense crowd little by little, almost furtively, until she was within reach of the Master. When she was close enough to reach him, she bent over with humility and faith and touched the hem of his garment. Healing came into her body immediately.

A later passage tells of the same faith-impelled action on the part of large groups: "And when the men of that place had knowledge of him, they sent out into all that country round about, and brought unto him all that were diseased; and besought him that they might only touch the hem of his garment: and as many as touched were made perfectly whole" (Matt. 14:35–36).

We remember that the outer garment worn by men during Christ's earthly sojourn was a long one, reaching to the ground. Therefore, to touch the hem of the garment of a man's outer robe was actually to be touching that part of his personal effects farthest away from the heart, which is the literal and figurative center of power in a person's life. Consequently, it is profoundly inspiring, even thrilling to recall that when people with deep needs in their lives touched him in the very "outposts" of his being, they found enough power there to meet those needs. Our Christ passed the "touch test" gloriously.

Every day people are touching the hem of the garment of your life and mine. They touch those sections of our lives which are normally farthest away from the center of church activity, or they touch *us* when we are under the normal pressures and tensions of the week. Do they find evidence of the living presence of Jesus in us regardless of when they touch us? Even

44

when we are neck-deep in swirling duties or tied up in knots of tension, do those who touch us find gentility, tenderness, patience, and a compassionate desire to help? Do they find us as inspiring when they touch our lives away from the church as we appeared to be when we taught that class, or made that talk, or sang in the choir loft? What happens to the needs and hungers in their lives when they touch the hem of the garment of your life?

There are four areas of living in which people are constantly touching the hem of the garment of our lives, four areas in which so many of us do not practice the Christianity which our lips have professed. Forgetting everybody else in the world, put yourself under the microscope, asking constantly, "What happens when problem-pressed people touch the hem of the garment of my life *at home, at work, at school, at leisure?*"

I

When we are within the four walls of home with the seeing eyes of the world not upon us, when we "let our hair down" and throw aside the restraints which have kept our real selves from being seen by the world, are we as attractive Christians there as the outside world thought us to be? Are we genuinely Christian in the quiet confines of home?

I touched the hem of the garments of two different men by visiting in their homes. Those experiences illustrate both the tragedy and the glory of the touch

45

test. The first man was a layman of wide usefulness in his church and community; in fact, he was the most sought-after lay speaker of that area. My impressions of him were not only favorable, they were quite enthusiastic. When we settled down for coffee and conversation in his living room, he gave vent to a long tirade of bitter criticism of a wide range of people, revealing that he was possessed of jealousy, arrogance, and pride. It was evident to me that there were real tensions between him and his family because of his domineering and thoughtless manner.

A wave of great disappointment swept over my heart, and I was almost sickened at this thought: What if I had been a younger, weaker, searching Christian, touching the hem of his garment, looking for strength and inspiration? I would have been disillusioned, if not actually embittered.

The second man in whose home I visited was also a church leader who, with his wife, exercised large influence upon the community. Though I had admired the family from seeing them often in public contact, I came to admire them more vastly when I discovered from a week-long visit that a spirit of gentility, tenderness, respect, and mutual thoughtfulness prevailed in the home. Though all the normal activity and rush of a family of five occurred during that week, this busiest man in a community of four thousand was a genteel Christian every hour within his own home. I touched the hem of the garment of his life in the four walls of home and found that he was more wonderful in his

Christianity than even his public performances had led me to believe.

II

When people come into contact with you in the place where you work and find you at your normal behavior, do they find your Christianity as vital as your Sunday behavior has indicated? Does the spirit of Christ characterize you throughout the working hours? Can the spirit of Christ be felt in your very atmosphere? Can he be seen in the radiance of your face? Can he be discovered in the convictions by which you live as you do your work? Can he be recognized in the compassions which you display and in the sympathies which you accord? What of the people who work with you, who rub shoulders with you every day: what do they think of your Christianity?

If, for one five-day week, the Christians of America would live their Christianity genuinely, winsomely, and comprehensively in the places where they work, a great religious transformation would occur. Millions would have touched the hem of the garment of Christian fellow workers and would have found a power there which could not be denied. Needs would be met, problems would be solved, questions would be answered, souls would be saved, and many nominal Christians would be brought to a closer walk with Jesus.

The manager of an automotive repair shop was a nominal Christian, but the twenty men who touched

47

the hem of his garment every work day surely felt no power there. Much bad talk and many wrong attitudes prevailed in the shop, largely because of the manager's failure to put Christian spirit and principle into his own relationships there. In a significant week-end revival meeting, this manager came back to a close walk with Jesus, much in the spirit of Peter after the denial experience. Power filled his life, even down to the hem of the garment!

Upon his return to work on Monday morning, he gathered his workmen about him. In a simple, straightforward manner he told them of the spiritual change which had come into his life since he saw them last. He explained that his reason for telling them immediately of the change was that they might understand why he would no longer participate in some of the conversations and attitudes which had prevailed in that shop. Then, with smiling assurance, he shared the testimony that he had been happier in the last forty-eight hours than at any time in his Christian experience. To the astonished workmen he suggested that they bow their heads for prayer before going to the morning tasks.

Silent astonishment was the first reaction as the men went about their respective tasks. Before the day had closed, several of them came to the young manager to ask further about his experience and to confess that they, too, had not been satisfied with their level of living. The climax of this very true story is that today in that same shop there is a spirit of complete transformation: work days begin with group prayer, conversation is entirely decent, and mutual concern for spiritual well-being is evident. "And," said the manager to me, "the efficiency of this shop has increased almost 100 per cent since we cleaned up our minds and hearts and came into step with Jesus."

You are just one stenographer among fifty people in an office, or just one clerk among a dozen in a store, or just one machine worker among a host of others in a factory, or just one employee anywhere in a situation which needs changing. What can one person do among so many? Of yourself, you can do little. Yet, if you are willing to pay the price of complete dedication to the spirit of Christ, you will be completely filled with his love, warmth, compassion, tenderness, radiance, and winsomeness. And the fellow workers who touch the hem of the garment of your life at work every day will find that you "have something" which makes you delightfully different, a something which some of them will want to possess. It won't work? I dare you to give Christ a chance through you!

III

If you are in school, people touch the hem of the garment of your life far more frequently than you realize. You were not even conscious that someone was looking at you during that terrific mathematics test last week and noticed that you declined help which was circulating up and down the row in which you sat. You weren't even conscious of the fact that someone passing in the hall overheard either a beautiful thing you said or a tart, unkind remark you made. It never occurred to you that anybody would give a second thought to the thoughtlessness you displayed in the cafeteria line, but somebody did!

So, I ask you frankly, student friend, what do fellow students think of your Christianity when they touch the hem of the garment of your life in the classroom, in the library, in the laboratory, in the corridors, on the athletic field? Do they think more or less of your Christianity from these contacts? If the students of your school were asked to list the five finest Christians they know, would your name be in the list?

I have visited on high school campuses where just one student has made a difference in an entire student body by living his Christianity comprehensively. I have known football teams whose spirit was transformed because one boy on the squad began to live so close to Jesus that when his fellows "touched the hem of his garment" they found genuine Christianity there. One student, living his or her Christianity everywhere and all the time, being touched by scores and hundreds of fellow students every day, can be used of God as the medium through which an entire student body can be made better. You could be that student in your school!

IV

There are Christians who fare reasonably well in the consistent living of their Christian principles in home, work, and school relationships, but who disappoint Christ in their social and recreational behavior. The disappointment comes generally from one of these mistakes: (1) Some Christians go to places and participate in activities which are out of harmony with the living presence of Jesus in their hearts. (2) Some Christians, while participating in activities which are entirely acceptable, behave in the wrong spirit. In view of the fact that the hems of the garments of our lives are being touched by so many people in our leisure-time activities, it becomes superlatively important that we be genuinely Christian even in our playtime hours.

Some teen-age boys, who were employed as attendants at a country club, told me with keen disappointment of two leaders in their church whom they had seen present in the club for cocktail parties, drinking alcoholic beverages. Their respect for those leaders had been lost and their confidence in them completely crushed—all from touching the hem of the garment of their lives in social activities of questionable nature.

A splendid young woman, recently won to Christ, was deeply disappointed in the ugly and, at times, vulgar conversations of some active church women who came to a select tea shop in which she worked as a waitress. A group of teen-age girls asked through the question box how they could help their Sunday school teacher to see that a certain social practice of her life was not thoroughly Christian. Several laymen told me that their enjoyment of an eloquent Sunday school teacher had been impaired because of their experiences with his poor sportsmanship on the golf course. Hems of garments!

During the days of my counseling on a college campus a student came to me with heated conviction, saying that he did not want ever again to hear another student (whom he named) make a religious talk. Upon inquiry, I discovered that he had double-dated with this student religious leader, and that, during the evening, the other boy had been definitely unchristian in his conversation and behavior. Hem touched. No power. Loss of confidence. Tragedy!

In the light of the strong possibility that some of us who have passed the touch test with credit on the first three counts may be unconsciously failing on this final count, every one of us can profitably re-examine *all* of his social and recreational activities in the light of these challenging passages: "Whether therefore ye eat, or drink, or whatsoever ye do, do all to the glory of God" (1 Cor. 10:31). "I am crucified with Christ: nevertheless I live; yet not I, but Christ liveth in me: and the life which I now live I live by the faith of the Son of God, who loved me, and gave himself for me" (Gal. 2:20). "For me to live is Christ, and to die is gain" (Phil. 1:21).

What happens when searching souls touch the hem of the garment of my life . . . or the hem of the garment of yours?

Oh, Righteous Father, we are frightened by the consciousness that many have touched us, seeking power, and have gone away disappointed. We are resolving now with all our hearts to live our Christianity so completely and comprehensively that whenever and wherever the searching ones touch our lives, there will be power there. But we must have thy power to sustain us. Do give to us that indispensable power in unending measure. Amen.

Five

The Crucible Test

"The Lord gave, and the Lord hath taken away; blessed be the name of the Lord." Job 1:21

"I can do all things through Christ which strengtheneth me." Philippians 4:13.

THE TRUEST TEST OF A MOTOR'S PERFORM-
ance never occurs on the easy road; it occurs on the difficult stretches of the journey. The strength of a tree is
never revealed in the blowing of the mild spring winds,
but in the weight of the blizzard's ice and in the impact
of the hurricane's force. The caliber of a football team
is never proved in a game with midget opposition but,
rather, when the opposition is terrific. So, with life and
people, the crucible test is generally necessary to reveal
genuine strength, courage, unselfishness, dedication,
or the lack of them.

Long-time workers with various types of timber declare that they can tell, from the flame colors of burning logs, a great deal about the chemical content and
something about the rigidity of life of those logs before they were cast into the "crucible" for burning.
Discerning metalworkers can tell a great deal about
the content of any piece of metal when it is burned
to white heat, and they can actually forecast its dura-
bility. All of that is logical. It is logical, too, that an

individual whose life is tested by stress and strain will reveal, in the process of his suffering, much about his strength or weakness.

There are always some people, however, who never accept the crucible as a normal part of life. Though they admit readily that storms are a normal part of the weather scheme, that winter is an integral part of the season pattern, that tragedy is an indispensable part of the field of drama, that dark cords are an adornment of enriching worth to many woven patterns, they seem unwilling to recognize sorrows, sufferings, and disappointments as normal and vital components of an individual's life.

These seeing but undiscerning people need to take a good, deep look at life! This kind of look will bring all except the hopelessly obstinate ones through to this conclusion: If there can be no steel without the white heat of the blast furnace, if there can be no refined gold without the excruciating crucible, if there can be no scintillating diamonds without the infinitely painful process of cutting, if there can be no great statuary without the long months and years in which the marble is submitted to the sculptor's chisel, *there are some things in life which will never come to an individual nor through that individual to the world by any other route than the crucible route.*

In view of the inevitability and inescapability of sorrows, sufferings, and disappointments, the individual will be wise to equip himself with a philosophy by which he can be sure to turn life's adversities into victory. Perhaps this philosophy can be reduced to a formula, hidden away in the individual's heart, held in readiness for quick use. I believe that this formula consists of three "musts."

I

The individual *must* be anchored to God. This anchoring begins, of course, with personal faith in Jesus Christ, but it will not be adequate anchorage if the Christian has not laid deeper and deeper hold upon God. This deepening hold will include a perpetually growing faith, an increasing possession of God's Word, a maturing prayer power, and a growing surrender of total self to the will of God. Many Christians do not bear up well in the crucible test—not because they are not anchored to God in faith, but because the initial anchoring which brought salvation has not been developed into mature consecration.

II

As quickly as the crucible experience comes, the Christian should exercise dynamic faith in God. In the immediacy and completeness of this kind of faith, the suffering Christian can find in Job a wonderful example. Before Job had any insight into why catastrophes had been heaped upon him, he looked up through the shambles of his broken life with the faith-filled declaration, "The Lord gave, and the Lord hath taken away; blessed be the name of the Lord."

One does not have to wait until the reasons for sufferings are made plain. If he has genuine faith in God, there are some declarations which he can make immediately. A Christian into whose life a staggering blow has come can say even through his numbness: "I *know* that God is good, that he is wise, that he is all-powerful, that he is tender and merciful, and I *know* that he loves me. I do not know that he sent this experience; for, indeed, it may well be that my own negligence or weakness has brought it; or, it may be that in this instance I am the victim of some other person's failure or sin. But this I do know: If God sent this experience, he sent it for my chastening, strengthening, refining. He sent it as a blessing for which I shall be able to thank him some day. If he did not send this experience—even if my own failure is responsible for it—I know that he will still release to me his power to help me turn this experience into the best possible circumstance."

I stood with a wonderful Christian outside her cottage at four o'clock in the morning. We had just driven back from a nearby hospital in which her cherished only son, a six-year-old, had died. That, in itself, was a stunning blow, for he had died after an illness of only forty-eight hours. To her, however, the loss was even greater, for it was the third major sorrow in quick succession. So there stood this gallant, lonely heroine. From the firmament of her life, the last little star had twinkled and gone out; from the repertoire of her heart, the favorite melody had been so quickly snatched away. For her, from there on out, stretched a long and lonesome road.

Feeling that I must say something to lighten the load of sorrow, I suggested that she should not try in this hour of physical exhaustion and heartbreak to try to figure out the why of this experience. I suggested, too, that God would help her to understand sometime and that, meanwhile, he would surely give to her the strength which her weary life so much needed.

Those words of intended consolation had hardly fallen from my lips when she replied with words which thrilled me then and which have strengthened me in many hours since that time.

"I know what you are trying to say," she said. "But you don't need to say it. I know God so well and trust him so fully that even now I would not call my little son back into life if I could; for I have learned in these years that there are so many things worse than death. As great as is the hurt of my heart now, I *know* that God would not have permitted him to go away unless his going now were not less of sorrow than some future experience, had he lived. God's way is sometimes, for a time, a way of tears; but it is *always* the better way."

The dynamic faith of that great Christian woman is worthy of emulation in our lives, too, in the very first moments of the crucible call.

III

When the full scope of the sorrow or the full impact of the blow becomes evident, the Christian who desires victory must accept the situation with intelligent surrender. Stoical fatalism, whining resignation, or the martyr complex will never bring God's victory to the Christian faced with a terrific experience. Nothing short of the intelligent surrender demonstrated by Christ in Gethsemane will suffice: "O my Father, if it be possible, let this cup pass from me: nevertheless not as I will, but as thou wilt" (Matt. 26:39).

It would be entirely unrealistic for the Christian to say that he is delighted that the tragedy has come to him, or for him to fail to try valiantly to avoid or alleviate the blow. Evidently, Christ did not prefer the cross to all other ways; yet, he was completely surrendered to death on it when he was faced with the fact that it was the only hope of atonement for the sins of the world. Similarly, when the Christian finds that the crucible of sorrow, defeat, or heartbreak is inescapable, he assures his victory by practicing that sort of intelligent surrender.

The Christian, practicing such surrender, will say, "O my Father, though I had not wished to take a role in a tragedy, I am willing to accept it and to do my best with it, if in the wisdom of thy will I can be best used in that manner. Though I have been horrified at the thought of blindness, or deafness, or lameness, or total invalidity of physical strength, I am willing to accept either or all of those infirmities if thou canst bless someone through me as thou didst through Fanny Crosby, Helen Keller, and a concourse of other noble ones. Remembering, O God, that thou hast ample power to turn tragedies into triumphs, I surrender myself to thee for guidance, power, and victory."

You have probably seen a violinist preparing to perform. He turns the keys which control the violin strings until the strings are stretched to the breaking point. We recognize that this tautness is imperative, for beautiful violin music cannot be played on strings which are not so stretched. Too, there are times in which our heartstrings may be stretched to the breaking point, so that we feel that one more hour of the grief will break us. If we are wise in those hours of taut heartstrings, we shall surrender them to the bow of God's will; and, wonderful to say, he will invariably play out of surrendered heartstrings, stretched to the breaking point, the most exquisite music of a lifetime.

From the blindness of John Milton came his richest literary compositions. From the imprisonment of John Bunyan came *Pilgrim's Progress*. Three successive failures and nine months of illness brought a young businessman to discover an idea which brought success and fame to a chain of stores bearing his name. From the poverty of many artists and from the privations of many scientists have come many of the world's richest art objects and many of its most serviceable inventions. Through Christ's death on the horrible cross and his victory over the forbidding grave came the greatest gift which the world has ever received. The principles of these glorious victories through the crucible of suffering are applicable to every vicissitude with which life may confront us.

Anchored to God, practicing intelligent faith and full surrender, the Christian may walk forward into the future unafraid of the worst that life may bring. With the formula for victory in his heart, he can say with assurance.

"When I am called upon to rest for a while upon the couch of suffering, it is as I rest there that I realize as never before the imperative necessity of God's power and the complete desirability of the companionship of Jesus. So, thank God for hospital beds and invalid couches which give us more of God's power and which teach us to practice the presence of Christ!

"When I am called upon to walk through the dark valley, it is because of the darkness of the valley that I look so eagerly for the footprints of God's leadership. So, thank God for dark valleys which bring us to search for him and to follow him gladly!

"When I am called upon to look out at the world through the blinding mist of bitter tears, it is because of the rainfall of tears that I seek the rainbow of God's promise. So, thank God for rainfall which brings his rainbow!"

We *can* pass the crucible test, for the promise of Philippians 4:13 is filled with God's truth and power: "I can do all things through Christ which strengtheneth me."

We are so grateful, Heavenly Father, that thou art adequate for the very worst that may ever befall us. Emboldened by the sure knowledge that thou art able and eager to help us to total victory, may we face even the crucible test with new and fuller surrender. Amen.

Six

The Hardest Test

*"But I say unto you, love your ene-
mies, bless them that curse you, do
good to them that hate you, and pray
for them which despitefully use you,
and persecute you."* Matthew 5:44.

IN THE TEACHINGS OF CHRIST IN THE WON-
derful fifth chapter of Matthew there is a refrain which
is filled with significant challenge: "Ye have heard that
it was said . . . But I say unto you. . . ." In every instance in which this refrain occurs, there is a challenge
to Christ's followers which carries this impact: "Up to
now, you have been considered to be excellent religion-
ists, beyond reproach in character and conduct, if you
went to this particular length; but now that you are
my followers, I want you to go farther than that."

For instance, he knew that they had been well taught
to refrain from committing murder. He knew, too, that
they regarded themselves to be murderers only when
they had actually killed someone. But he wanted them
to abstain not only from the act of killing; he wanted
them to abstain even from the conditions of mind and
heart out of which murder arises. He knew that they
had been equally well taught to abstain from adultery,
and that they thought themselves free from the taint

of immorality if they merely refrained from the act. He, however, asked them to refrain from both the deed and the lustful thoughts which often lead to it. In short, he wished his followers to go farther than *doing* right in conduct: he wanted them to *be* right in character.

Verses 43–48 of this fifth chapter of Matthew contain teachings of Jesus which, for many Christians, present the hardest test to which they are ever put. To fulfil the challenge of those verses necessitates putting self completely under the thumb and putting the spirit of Christ completely on the throne of one's heart. The accomplishment of the ideals set forth in those verses will amount to a literal crucifixion of selfishness, a real enthronement of Christ in the emotional life, and an inevitable transformation of one's relationships to other people. It is a high hurdle test. The Christian who passes this test must be able not only to run as it were a race but to jump over hurdles of self as he runs. In these six significant verses there are at least three ways in which Jesus wants his followers to go farther.

I

"But I say unto you, love your enemies." *He expects us to go farther in applying the principle of love.* More than nineteen hundred years after Christ taught this new length for the application of love, there are multitudes of his followers who have not caught its meaning or who are not willing to practice its challenge. They go right along loving only the attractive and lovable ones, reciprocating affection, but never bestowing the gift of love upon those who are difficult to love. Most of all, these followers have failed even to *try* to love the people who are their personal enemies.

When the import of "love your enemies" begins to dawn upon the average Christian, his reaction may range all the way from astonishment to rebellion. Argues the average Christian: "Lord, you do not really mean that you expect me to love that person whose long, loose tongue has damaged my reputation—or the one who defrauded me, bruised my feelings, trampled my emotions—and surely not that particular person who is mean, conniving, sniveling, fawning in my presence, stabbing me in the back. Why, Lord, he is not just offensive; he is absolutely repulsive. Surely, you do not mean these people, Lord." If the inquirer pauses long enough to let his blood pressure subside and his emotions calm down, he will feel the answer of Jesus in his heart: "But I say unto you, love those people, too."

The Christian will take his first step in going farther in applying the principle of love if he can disassociate the word "love" from the caressing and kissing connotation with which American usage has freighted it. The quality of love which Jesus had in mind is Christian love, the essence of which is the capacity to look at a person through the eyes and heart of Christ. When one looks at an unfortunate person, even one's enemy, through Christ's eyes and heart, he will see so many things which a look through the selfish eyes of mere human love would not reveal.

The world looked at the adulterous woman who was dragged into Christ's presence, at Zaccheus, at the woman of Sychar and heaped condemnation, scorn, and ignominy upon them. Christ looked at the same persons through the loving heart of God, whom they had so sorely offended, and he saw in them qualities and possibilities not discernible to the vain, selfish eyes of the world. He loved them, not for what they were, but for what they could be when, through the power of God, they were released from the dreadful sins which made them reprehensible.

To see sinful people in this fashion, particularly the ones whose sins have hurt us personally, requires a constant swallowing of our own vanity, false pride, and selfishness. Until we cease to look at our enemies through our own eyes, we can never begin to love them. When we begin to see them through the eyes and heart of Christ, the normal human emotions of resentment and hate will be displaced by pity, grief, and compassion for the persons whose sins have hurt both them and us. A significant number of American soldiers who were submitted to months and years of indignity in Japanese prisoner-of-war camps looked at their captors in this spirit and, wonderful to say, they came through with so much Christian love for their enemies that some have gone back to Japan as missionaries.

Regardless of seriousness of the wrong done to you

70

and me by someone else, at its worst it will never approach the depravity of the wrong done to Christ by his enemies. At the height of his suffering on the cross, he looked out upon the still-reviling enemies and demonstrated Christian love to its ultimate in praying, "Father, forgive them; for they know not what they do." By comparison, how little are the wrongs done to us, and how little many of us practice the principle of Christian love to the wrongdoers!

With the wonderful example of Jesus in extending the principle of love to encompass even his enemies, with the very clear teaching of Jesus which bids us to do likewise, and with the very real promise of his power to help us, we are very poor followers, indeed, if we do not try until we have succeeded in going farther in Christian love—so far, in fact, that even the hardest-to-love enemy is warmly encompassed in the circle of our love.

II

". . . And pray for them which despitefully use you." *Jesus expects us to go farther in forgiveness,* for we cannot pray genuinely and effectually for those whom we have not forgiven. To forgive those who have despitefully used us and persecuted us is to take the principle of forgiveness to new lengths. In the matter of forgiveness, Jesus pointed out some ways in which he wants us to go farther.

First, he wants us to forgive without "number limit." One of his disciples asked if we should forgive a brother seven times. To this question Jesus replied, "Until seventy times seven." The clear implication is that we are Christ-bound to forgive as long as the offender asks with repentance for forgiveness. Throughout his teachings there are many reminders to his followers that they be generous in forgiveness, that they forgive others as generously and graciously as God has forgiven them.

Second, he taught through his example on the cross that we can forgive even before our offenders ask us for forgiveness. Probably, the most remote thought in the minds of the revilers around the cross was the thought of asking for forgiveness; yet, Jesus indicated in the immortal "Father, forgive them" that he had already forgiven them in his own heart. Therefore, the sinned-against Christian need not wait for the offender to come to ask forgiveness; he can provide it right now! And if the offender never comes to ask forgiveness, God can see that the Christian's heart had provided the package of forgiveness, wrapped in love, tied with the bow of friendship, and offered in the grace of humility.

Third, Christ taught that we ought to take the initiative in working out reconciliation with people who have wronged us. This amounts to providing the forgiveness and taking it to the offender. This is, indeed the ultimate in forgiveness! Matthew 5:23–24 presents this new length to which forgiveness should be taken: "Therefore if thou bring thy gift to the altar, and there rememberest that thy brother hath ought against thee;

leave there thy gift before the altar, and go thy way; first be reconciled to thy brother, and then come and offer thy gift."

An active church member told me of her sorrow that another woman in that community seemed to have a deep dislike, if not active resentment toward her. She was very insistent in declaring that she had done absolutely nothing to offend the other woman and that she was at a total loss to understand the antagonistic attitude. When I asked if she proposed to do anything about the situation, she replied with noticeable warmth: "Me? Why, of course not. I have done nothing to wrong her; the bad attitude is her own fault. It is her duty to come to me if she is offended." Then, indicating unmistakably that her own heart was not free from resentment, she said heatedly of the other woman, "She can just sizzle in her own grease, so far as I am concerned!"

I read to her the challenge of Matthew 5:23–24 and suggested that before she came back to her church to offer her gift of service as a Sunday school teacher, she ought to obey that teaching of Christ. It has been my high privilege to suggest a similar course of action to many Christians. Some of them have followed the suggestion with results which brought power and joy to them. Even in cases in which the other person involved would not be reconciled, the Christian who "went farther" came away from the experience with peace of heart and a new sense of nearness to Jesus.

We cannot afford not to go farther in forgiveness.

We not only grieve God in our failure to go farther, we rob our fellows of a demonstration of Christian forgiveness, and we limit God's forgiveness toward us. The message of Matthew 6:14–15 needs no commentary: "For if ye forgive men their trespasses, your heavenly Father will also forgive you: But if ye forgive not men their trespasses, neither will your Father forgive your trespasses." It is to be hoped most earnestly that we shall never again pray "Forgive us our debts, as we forgive our debtors" without resolving to go farther in forgiveness!

After I had spoken fervently in an early morning meeting, one time, upon the Christian's obligation to love and forgive, a lady came to me with noticeable agitation of spirit. She told me of vicious things which her neighbor had said about her, indicating that the neighbor had spread the false reports quite widely. The farther she went in the recital of her neighbor's sin against her, the more indignant she became.

"I don't love her, I can't love her, and I don't believe that God expects me to try to love a woman as wicked as she," declared the wounded victim.

As quietly as possible, I clothed many of the ills which were said about Christ and which were done to him in modern situations and terminology and asked, "Has your neighbor said this about you yet . . . or has she done this to you yet?" Of course, her answers had to be a succession of negative replies. Then I pointed out that her Christ, who had been the recipient of immeasurably more wrong from so many more

74

people, had not only not reacted with her type of bitterness but had, on the contrary, actually prayed for his enemies as he died on the cross.

There dawned upon this embittered Christian the tragic truth that she had behaved as badly toward an enemy as if she had never belonged to Jesus. There came quick conviction that she needed to do two things: to sweep her own heart clean of hatred for a personal enemy, and to take the initiative in trying to convey Christian love and forgiveness to this enemy. She spent much time in prayer that day, but she came through with hatred put out of her heart, and with Christlike love and forgiveness brought in.

Then she went out to her garden, picked a pail full of tender beans, called her neighbor to the back fence. The neighbor, weighed down by her consciousness of wrong was reluctant to come, and still more reluctant to accept the green beans, until the neighbor overwhelmed her with the full explanation of the meaning of the offer.

"You know how I have felt toward you because of the many evil things which you have said about me. I feel that, in God's sight, you have done a great wrong to me. Yet, I have been wrong to the degree that I permitted myself to hate you for your injustices toward me. This morning, however, I have confessed my sin of hatred; God has forgiven me; I have forgiven you, and I have brought this token with my own hands to say that, though you must still settle the matter of your sin with God, my heart is free of any malice toward you. Anything which a Christian can do for another, I am so willing to do for you."

The neighbor who had committed the great sin of vicious gossip was so touched by the spirit of Christ in her neighbor that she wept with genuine contrition. A wonderful reconciliation occurred with great joy to both women, because one Christian had gone farther in loving and forgiving.

III

"Do good to them that hate you." *Christ expects us to go farther in serving*. In fulfilling the obligation to serve, many of us behave in a fashion so similar to the world that Christ is justified in his asking, "What do ye more than others? Do not even the publicans so?" We are inclined to serve only those who are worthy, those who are expressive of appreciation, those who reciprocate, those who are our friends. We need to face the stark truth: the unregenerate person, the pagan, and the heathen can do that well in serving. Surely, the follower of Jesus can and must do better, go farther in service to fellow man than the unchristian world goes.

If Christ had served only the worthy ones, none would have been served. If he had served only those who thanked him, he would have reduced his healing of lepers by 90 per cent, for only one out of ten came back to thank him. If he had served only those who reciprocated, his service life would have been negligible. If he had served only his friends, few of the five

76

thousand would have been fed that day. He operated on a principle of service vastly different from the principles which impelled his world: He kept his eyes on God, he looked at people and their needs through the loving heart of God, and he kept on serving as long as he felt that God would have him serve.

At Christmastime, so many Christians of us reveal that we have not begun to catch the spirit of Christ in giving and serving. The average Christian sits down to make his Christmas list with this dominant question in his heart, "To whom do I owe gifts this Christmas?" Starred on that list are those to whom he has obligations or those from whom he anticipates gifts and favors.

Off the list go people who didn't give to him last Christmas; for those who give only erratically, there are listed provisional gifts—gifts laid by "just in case." For those who gave gifts last Christmas, there are listed gifts to the carefully calculated amount probably put into the gifts received, generous gifts for generous givers and penurious gifts for the little givers. And, tragic to say, the same spirit actuates the average Christian's giving and serving all year!

We need to follow the spirit of Jesus in serving. We need to take our eyes off ourselves and off the people who need to be served and to look only at their need through the loving heart of Christ. Perhaps the people who need to be served are not worthy, but Christ is worthy. Perhaps the people who need to be served are not grateful, reciprocative, or even friendly, but Christ

77

is grateful for my service to the ones who need to be served. He will fill my cup to overflowing with compensating joys, because I have fed his sheep. He is my friend and will glow with happiness and approval because I have displayed his spirit toward unworthy, ungrateful, unreciprocating, and unfriendly people. Until we dedicate ourselves to rendering service in his name, in his spirit, for his sake, and to his lengths, we shall neither go as far as we ought to go in Christian service, nor derive as much joy from it.

How does your life stand up to this three-fold hardest test?

Oh, Father, we have been so much like our world and so little like our Lord in loving, forgiving, and serving. But we do want to be better, to go farther. Therefore, do help us to rise above the selfishness of our hearts and the habit of conforming to our world. Help us to go farther for Christ's sake, for our sake, and for the sake of others who will be blessed through us. Amen.

Seven

Addition

"And beside this, giving all diligence, add to your faith virtue; and to virtue knowledge; and to knowledge temperance; and to temperance patience; and to patience godliness; and to godliness brotherly kindness; and to brotherly kindness charity." **2 Peter** 1:5–7.

IF YOU HAVE NOT HAD THE EXPERIENCE personally, you have been very near someone into whose family a child had just been born. You will remember with nostalgia the eagerness with which the young parents watched for even the tiniest evidence of physical and intellectual growth on the child's part. Every ounce added in weight, every inch added in height, every new indication of recognition and response brought thrills to the devoted parents' hearts. Growth failure in either physical or mental areas would have precipitated quick trips to pediatricians and psychiatrists. Permanent failure to grow in either area would have been marked down as stark tragedy.

A host pastor and I had been luncheon guests in a home whose only child had the physical size and mental level of a twelve-year-old. There were two or three factors which led me to believe that she was older in years than twelve; therefore, as we drove away, I asked the minister about the case. He told me a sad story, indicating that at twelve years of age she had become a victim of a peculiar succession of illnesses, one of which had arrested her physical growth, another of which had arrested her mental growth. Then I understood more fully the evident pathos and compassionate sorrow in the faces of the two devoted parents.

As I sat in contemplation immediately thereafter, there came this strong impression into my heart: as sad as is the case of arrested physical and mental growth, it is vastly more sad that our Heavenly Father is obliged to look down upon so many of his children who have just deliberately chosen to continue to be spiritual infants or spiritual dwarfs! It occurred to me, further, that his sadness must be even deeper than that of the earthly parents, because he knows that the circumstances which have caused us to be infants and midgets are within our control and that we can resume spiritual growth and continue it through life if we honestly want to grow.

Seven "additions" or aspects of total spiritual growth which every Christian life should experience are listed in 2 Peter 1:5–7. As we look now into that list, it will be helpful for each of us to ask himself some questions concerning each of these facets of growth. Am I doing better in *that* way than I did a year ago? Much better than five years ago? In which of these seven ways am I still in the cradle or just toddling?

I

To faith, which was all we had the moment we were born again, we are asked, first, to add *virtue*. Our English word "virtue" comes directly from the Latin *virtus,* the chief meaning of which is strength. Therefore, first in the list of additions to the life of the newly born Christian is strength. Just as the baby adds strength to turn over, to sit alone, to stand and walk alone, and eventually to carry loads and to perform large tasks, the growing Christian should be perpetually adding spiritual strength. What kinds of strength should the Christian be adding?

The growing Christian should be increasing in faith, believing in God more fully and implicitly, believing God's Word to the point of obeying it minutely and joyously, trusting more and more of one's life to God's will, believing Christ so literally and following his teachings so faithfully that he, like Paul, can say, "For me to live is Christ." Do you *know* that your faith in God, in God's word, in Jesus Christ, in the Holy Spirit, is stronger today than a year ago?

There are other kinds of spiritual strength which should appear with increasing evidence in the growing Christian's life. He should be stronger in his hold upon God's Word from reading it much, believing it joyously, and translating it victoriously into his own life. He should be stronger in prayer, stronger in conviction, stronger in his desire and capacity to worship and to serve, stronger in his compassion for lost people, and stronger in his ability to take life's reverses with a victorious spirit.

A seventeen-year-old boy became a Christian. No one else in his family was a Christian and none attended church. This new Christian began to add strength immediately. His prayer life grew so rapidly and with such power that within three months he was praying with the maturity of a Christian of many years experience, proving to himself and others that prayer changes things. His faithful study of God's Word brought such deepening conviction that he was able to "stand his ground" victoriously in his family and in school contacts. His faith increased to the point that he believed that some "impossible" people could be reached for Christ. In less than one year after his own conversion, he had won two members of his family and several of his closest associates. When I visited in his church ten months after he became a Christian, he was highly regarded as the outstanding young Christian of his city.

How does your present spiritual strength compare with your strength of last year? Is your spiritual strength as large and vital as it should be in the light of the length of time in which you have been a Christian? Are you able to stand alone and walk alone now, or are you still depending largely upon other people for guidance and strength? Are you making progress toward the time in which you will be strong enough to be a giver of strength to others?

II

Second in the list of spiritual additions is *knowledge*. Any observer of a small child will agree that the amount of knowledge added by that child in one year is amazing; in five years, phenomenal! Once, I rode for six hours just one seat behind a mother and her six-year-old son, who was experiencing his first train ride. Your imagination can supply the intriguing details of the mother-son conversation. It seemed to me that his questions must have averaged one a minute. In his vast interrogation, he covered the whole field of trains, their operation, the conductors and flagmen and porters, the manipulation of the seats and foot-rests, and so forth, *ad infinitum!* When he wearied of questions concerning the interior of the train, he quizzed his mother concerning objects along the trainside.

When we arrived at our destination, I breathed a quiet prayer of gratitude that the lad belonged to her and not to me, for I would have been humiliated by the number of his questions which I could not have answered. Once I was far enough removed to breathe comfortably—for I had secretly feared that the distraught mother might turn at any moment to ask me the answer to some of his perplexing questions—I made this mental note: that lad had garnered more general knowledge in six hours than the average Christian gains of spiritual knowledge in six years. His knowledge increased because he had an appetite to learn and because he made an effort to learn.

Have you added the amount of spiritual knowledge which the years of your Christian experience have made possible? Do you know more about God? Do you know him not only as the righteous judge, but also as the tender father who loves you so and is interested in you to the degree of having even the hairs of your head numbered? Do you know more about Jesus Christ? You know him as Saviour; but do you know him, too, as the elder brother, as the friend who sticketh closer than a brother, as the constant companion, as the answer to all of your needs? Do you know the Holy Spirit through personal experiences in which his unmistakable power directed and empowered you?

Do you *know* that faith is the victory? Can you cite instances from your life in which faith has brought victory? Do you *know* that prayer changes things? What has it changed in you and through you? Do you *know* that it pays to serve Jesus? Did you learn that truth from hearsay or "do-say"? Do you *know* that surrender pays incomparable dividends, because you have practiced surrender to the will of God? Do you *know* that God's Word is the all-sufficient guide to human conduct, because you have permitted it to be that sort of guide for you?

III

"And to knowledge temperance . . ." This third facet of growth, *temperance,* has suffered in America because of its almost exclusive connection with the problem of liquor drinking. To the average American the use of the word temperance implies either moderation or abstinence in the matter of alcoholic beverages; whereas, actually, in its origin the word has no closer connection with liquids than with solids, no more allusion to materials than to emotions, attitudes, and general appetites. Therefore, in its truest application temperance is life-wide. Many who have never tasted liquor are intemperate in thought, tongue, temper, food. Many who have never been intoxicated by alcohol are frequently intoxicated in heart by spite, malice, envy, jealousy, resentment, hatred, and the unforgiving spirit.

Children lack the power of reason and, therefore, demonstrate little temperance in some important areas of life. Without guidance from elders they would eat much of some rich delicacies and little of important body-building foods; they would eliminate naps and early-to-bed regulations; they would have as little as possible to do with soap and water. Their lack of judgment and their need to have their lives "tempered" by wise guidance from others can be viewed as normal during their early years. The failure to develop a "tempering judgment" to guide themselves as they grow older, however, is cause for deep alarm. The older one becomes, the more evident in his life should be the tempering power of good judgment.

Temperance applied to the Christian's whole personality ought to mean that Christ is the control tower of life through the Christian's complete surrender and that Christ, therefore, is permitted to control and rein in any part of life which tends to run out of control. Thus, Christ in control will temper one's thinking, speaking, temper, emotions, attitudes, appetites. In this concept the Christian is temperate to the degree to which Christ controls his life. If Christ-control widens and deepens through the years, the Christian is becoming more truly temperate.

IV

The fourth proof-positive of spiritual growth, as pictured in this list, is *patience*. Patience is not a child's virtue. A child lacks a sense of values and a sense of time; therefore, he does not have the capacity to wait with grace and forbearance. As he grows in years, however, he normally learns both a sense of values and a sense of time which enable him to accept with finer calm of spirit the things which would have upset him and the delays which would have enraged him in his infancy.

We had sat down for lunch in a home in which there was a five-year-old son. He had waited with some measure of calm while the guests were being seated and while the blessing was said. Immediately thereafter, however, he looked across at his mother and announced impatiently, "I want my apple pie right now!"

The mother, not meaning for her dessert to be announced that early in the meal, frowned her disapproval, and the father dissuaded; but the five-year-old, unable to wait graciously for a helping of the good pie which he had seen his mother preparing, wanted his helping right then. There was a sudden flash of memory of my childhood which caused me to smile at the little boy's impatience. In my childhood, it seemed to me that the adults consumed an interminable amount of time between soup and dessert, and I thought that we would never get around to the freshly frozen ice cream!

Without a sense of values, time or propriety, the five-year-old had neither the capacity nor inclination to wait patiently. His lack of patience was fully understandable. When he is even five years older, however, he can be expected to demonstrate more of patience; when he is thirty-five, he ought to be a master in the art of waiting graciously.

There is no surer proof of growing spiritual maturity than the Christian's development of patience. This development will proceed to limits of great maturity if the Christian tries faithfully to appraise everything and everybody through the eyes of Christ. Looking at circumstances through his eyes will give to us an understanding which, in turn, will help us to wait more graciously. Looking at people through his eyes will restrain our minds from condemnation and our tongues from quick criticism. In this technique, we shall come to the point of waiting more patiently for God's will to work out, for our prayers to be answered, for other people to "grow up," and for our own spiritual strength to develop gradually.

The Christian who gives himself to bursts of impatience is suffering a three-fold hurt: psychologically, he is agitated unduly; physiologically, he reacts with excitement which he can actually feel; and spiritually, his heart reproves him for the lack of kindness which real patience always carries. Furthermore, one burst of impatience may hurt another or others seriously. What if Christ had given himself to a burst of impatience toward Peter because of his vigorous denial of his Lord? From hurt, disappointment, and discouragement Peter might have been lost to the Christian ministry. As Christ looked down upon Pentecost, he must have been profoundly happy that he had been infinitely patient toward Peter!

V

The three final marks of spiritual growth are an inseparable triumvirate, for one cannot achieve the first of the three without achieving the other two logically. First in this triumvirate is *godliness*, which means essentially the state of being like our Father, God.

How often have you heard people say of some little one, "He is just the living image of his father"? Did they mean to be saying that the baby and its father looked just alike right then? Quite naturally not! They did mean to be saying, though, that the main traits of appearance in the little one had such marked similarities to those of his father that anybody who knew the father would recognize the son. It is surely true that if a child is going to resemble his father noticeably, there will be some little traits of similarity evident in the first days of its life. Naturally, the older the child becomes, the more like its father it will be.

During the very first days of our Christian experience there should be characteristics of living which would enable anyone who knows our Heavenly Father to say, "I know whose child you are, for you resemble your Father definitely." As we grow older in our Christian experience, the more like our Heavenly Father we ought to become in compassion, conviction, courage, consistency, and consecration—so much like him that people who do not even know our names or backgrounds will recognize our parentage.

Brotherly kindness is an inevitable result of godliness. God so loved fallen man that he gave his choicest possession for man's redemption. Christ, being like his Father, so loved that he wept over stubborn Jerusalem. His heart burned within him out of compassion as he looked upon the multitudes, and his surrendered spirit was willing to suffer the death of the cross for man's atonement.

As soon as Andrew became a child of God through faith in Jesus, he yearned to introduce his brother, Simon Peter, to him. As soon as Paul came to be God's son through redemption, he yearned with an almost inexpressible longing to share with his fellow Jews the love of God through Christ. Down through the centuries, a great galaxy of men and women, becoming more like their Heavenly Father, have had hearts literally burning with love and concern for the spiritual needs of their brothers throughout the world.

If I am becoming more like my Father, God, I, too, shall come to look upon the needs of brother-men, yearning for their salvation, longing to meet all the needs of their lives it is possible for me to meet. If there is not that unmistakable longing in my heart to feed the Master's sheep, there is missing from my life an

indispensable by-product of godliness, brotherly kindness.

Brotherly kindness always eventuates in *charity*.
Charity is the word which I speak with my lips or the
deed which I do with my hands because brotherly kindness impelled it; and the brotherly kindness had come
to be the atmosphere of my heart because of my increasing likeness to my Father, God. Out of the life of
the godly Christian will flow unending streams of service.

I knew a seminary student whose financial means
were extremely limited. From the small amount of
compensation which a little rural church gave to him,
he had to pay his bus fare to and from the appointment. He noticed people in the bus station in need of
both clothing and food. The Christlike spirit of brotherly kindness so filled his heart that he began the practice of using his bus-fare money to purchase food and
some clothing for these people, while he would "hitch
hike" rides to his appointment. Then he capitalized
upon the free ride by telling his traveling companions
about Jesus. Nobody who touches his life will ever
doubt that this wonderful person is truly a child of
God!

In the light of a frequent re-reading of these powerful, pungent verses, 2 Peter 1:5–7, let us step onto the
scales to see if we are adding the spiritual weight which
the growing Christian ought to add; let us stand under
the measuring stick to see if we are achieving the
spiritual growth which Christ expects, which our lives

need, and which our world will not fail to notice and respect.

Imbue us, O God, with the desire to get out of our bassinets and play pens in which so many of us have chosen to live in the realm of the spiritual. Shame us deeply that we have lived in the nursery so long. Touch us with resolution and courage to grow up. Amen.

Eight

Subtraction

"Wherefore laying aside all malice, and all guile, and hypocrisies, and envies, and all evil speakings . . . that ye may grow. . . ." 1 Peter 2:1–2.

"When I was a child, I spake as a child, I understood as a child, I thought as a child: but when I became a man, I put away childish things." 1 Corinthians 13:11.

You AND I WILL AGREE THAT THERE IS NO
sound this side of heaven any sweeter than the sound of
a little child lisping his first words. "Ma-ma, Da-da,"
falling from those little lips contain music, love, and
thrills for a whole family. Yet, if that same baby-pro-
nunciation of words is continued into the teens, there
is the universal feeling of "What a tragedy!"

It is right and heart-warming for a baby to talk like
a baby, to play like a baby, to act like a baby. But, as
this child grows up, one of the surest proofs of its
growth is that it lays aside its baby talking, baby
clothes, and baby habits. One of the surest indications
that a child is wanting to grow up is that he begins to
imitate grown people's habits.

In the process of spiritual growth, too, it is normal
that in our earliest experiences inevitable immaturities
of attitude and behavior appear; but it is also normal
that the growing Christian lay aside these immature
and inappropriate characteristics—traits which can be
viewed with patience and tolerance in one's "beginning-

97

to-walk" days but, if continued in the Christian's life, become hurtful to him and disappointing to others.

In my long years of visiting churches throughout America, I was first surprised and have since been deeply grieved to discover that the overwhelming majority of all unhappiness in church relationships arises out of adults who have not grown up spiritually. Some men on church boards act like five-year-old children: they insist on having their way, sulk if their requests are not honored, and, all too often, either leave the church or remain to obstruct its progress with "hurt child" behavior. Women give way to childish emotions of pride, jealousy, desire for attention. Choir members "get their feelings hurt" at the slightest imagined offense. Adults obstruct inevitable progress in grading systems because, like children, they are not willing to listen to logic nor to give a recommended system a fair trial. There are far more children clothed in adult bodies in our churches than there are in the nurseries—people who have been Christians for many years but who have not laid aside childish ways!

I

First Peter 2:1 lists five representative things which the growing Christian needs to lay aside or put away. The first of these matters to be subtracted from the Christian's life is *malice*. More than that, the writer of that passage directs that we lay aside all malice.

In its first dealings with his world, the child has nothing to guide him except his own bundle of feelings.

Reason is undeveloped; there is no sense of time, value, or respect. It is normal, therefore, for the child to react to hurt or frustration in the most primitive response: to cry out in rebellion and to fight back in resentment.

Patsy was five years old, sprightly, and spoiled! When I arrived for a short visit, she insisted upon going through all the drills which she had learned in play school, most of the drills being little short of physical contortions. Her mother insisted that she stop her over-activity, because there were several cherished lamps on various tables in the living room. Patsy heard but did not choose to obey. Shortly thereafter she bumped the table on which the most cherished lamp stood, and only her mother's agility saved the lamp from crashing to the floor.

Patsy's mother immediately whisked her to the kitchen and administered a spanking as a reward for her disobedience. As Patsy seethed back through the living room, she was aflame with malice, for her feelings had been hurt both figuratively and literally. In a vigorous outburst, she declared: "When I get to be a big girl, I'm going a long way from home. I'm going out to Texas; and if my mother comes after me, I'll lock the screen door so she can't get in!"

Reason, respect for other people, desire for group approval, and the "for Jesus' sake" motivations were beyond her current development. Hence, the malicious expression and action on her part were perfectly normal. Growth in years, wise parental guidance, and a genuine experience with Jesus have led Patsy to the discovery that malice of heart or action is both unwise and unchristian. She is today a lovely teen-age Christian with all malice laid aside.

Malice is to be distinguished from the normal feelings of disagreement, dislike, and resentment, for these feelings may occur with justification when principle has been violated. Even these normal emotional reactions may grow into malice, however, if they are permitted to linger in the heart. Even the person who has been greatly wronged can cherish feelings of hurt and resentment so long and warmly that there will arise an inevitable wish that hurt may come to the wrongdoer.

You may feel, perhaps, that the wrong done to you by someone is so vicious and so entirely unjustified that it is asking the impossible to ask that you relinquish all feelings of malice. If that is your feeling, you will do well to sit down soon to recount all the venomous things said and done against our Christ, remembering that not one of those evil things was deserved by him. Yet, greatly sinned against and entirely innocent, suffering the horror of death on the cross, he revealed that his heart was completely free of malice. He went farther than that: He even prayed that God would forgive his persecutors! He would have been immeasurably more justified in harboring malice than would any one of us. It becomes surpassingly tragic, therefore, that anyone who has belonged to Jesus over a period of years should retain any malice in his heart!

"But I have no malice in my heart toward anybody," some reader is saying. Let everyone of us look again, each into the privacy of his own heart. If there is even a trace of jealousy, envy, covetousness, personal dislike, or the unforgiving spirit, there is ample material from which the stuff of malice grows. The wise Christian will stamp out the embers now, lest the fire of malice spring up later.

II

Though *guile* carries primarily the meaning of deception, we are regarding the word here as alluding to any sinful habit. The child's first experiences find him committing acts which, looked at through adult eyes, are theft and falsehood. The child's hands almost instinctively reach out to pick up things which appeal to him, not knowing that to take those things is to steal. Or, with the aid of a sprightly imagination, he reports elephants in the back yard when only large dogs are there. Without proper understanding and instruction, the child may commit those acts with no consciousness of wrong. Upon proper instruction and wise discipline, however, he can be expected to lay aside those practices. He goes against his better knowledge not to give them up.

The young Christian may easily commit acts which are out of harmony with his new life, not realizing the inconsistency and wrong involved. But the Christian who is old enough in mind to distinguish right from wrong, and who has followed Christ for long enough to develop both a Christian conscience and a love motivation to follow that conscience cannot defend his habitual sin with the plea, "I didn't know that it was wrong." If he speaks the whole truth, he will be obliged to say: "Knowing full well that it is wrong, I continue to do it because I do not love Christ sufficiently to lay aside this sin for his sake."

Do I mean to be saying that the time will come in this life in which you and I will have no sin in our lives? I do mean to be saying that the time ought to come in this life in which you and I will not have any *habitual* practice of wrong in our lives. All of us are susceptible to the impetuous and thoughtless wrong and to the honest mistake. In no life, however, will the sin be repeated to the habit stage without our knowledge and consent. The growing Christian has no alternative: he is asked to lay aside all guile.

III

One of the most normal traits of childhood is imitation. Didn't you pretend a great deal during your childhood? If you were a boy, you probably pretended to be a grocer, a fireman, an engineer, a bus driver—just as your younger brother or little son now pretends to pilot a space ship. You probably rode a broomstick, imagining with vigor that you were a cowboy riding a bucking bronco. If you were a girl, you doubtless dressed up in your mother's long dress and went through hours of pretended visiting, schoolteaching, and even child-spanking. Fancy yourself now, grown man that you are, riding a broomstick on your lawn. Or, grown woman that you are, sitting for hours on your living room floor, playing paper dolls. All of those imitations are a part of the psychology of childhood but would be regarded as marks of mental infirmity if perpetuated into adulthood.

The spiritual newborn may wisely follow the patterns of older, finer Christians—at first, even to the point of imitation. He needs to guard from the very beginning of his experience, however, against pretending to be what he is not, or to possess convictions or emotions which are not in his heart, or achievements of spiritual growth which he has not actually experienced.

God's attitude toward *hypocrisy* is graphically revealed in Matthew 23:27, in which verse hypocrites are called "whited sepulchres." The Christian may well and wisely pray, "Lord, help me to be genuine. Help me to be the same from the center of my heart to the fingertips of my life. Help me to be victorious over all artificiality and pretense. Deliver me from hypocrisy!"

IV

Psychologists are not surprised by the development of *envy* in the mind of one child when another child comes into the home. Since the child's world centers in itself, he is disturbed by the necessity of sharing love, attention, and gifts with the newcomer. He isn't old enough to understand that true parental love is so wonderful that there is more than enough to "go around" even if there were a dozen children in the family. With immaturity, inadequacy, and fear pressing down upon his childish mind, the child reacts with envy.

After the first days of excitement attendant upon her little brother's birth, Sandra began to develop strange symptoms—pretended illnesses; and her parents were actually alarmed until a discerning friend explained the normal factor of envy. Eight-year-old Bill called his father aside, in the first month of the life of his newly arrived sister, and advised his father with all seriousness, "Dad, our family is just getting to be too large." These indications of envy are the rule, not the exception with normal children. But with people who are old enough in years, mind, and spiritual development, envy ought to be the exception, not the rule.

For you or me to react toward other people with feelings of envy is both psychologically and spiritually childish. Envy indicates a lack of faith in God's plan; for his plan is so vast in scope and personal in nature that he needs every one of us vitally. Nobody can take your place or mine. The success of another person in your field does not mean that you are any less loved or needed in God's plan. Envy indicates a lack of faith in God's love. The envious person is acting as if the success or joy of another implies that God loves the other person more. With all other baby habits, envy ought to be laid aside.

V

When a little child first begins to talk, he simply reproduces mechanically the words which have come in through his ears from the conversations of other people. Generally, he does not have any idea of the meanings of those words. Consequently, if his lips speak some words which are not right, he is not as much to be blamed as are the people from whose conversations he heard the wrong words, or as he himself should be blamed when he later understands the full import of those words. Having grown up to a full consciousness of words and their meanings, the child can no longer make the defense, "I didn't know that those words were wrong."

Every Christian who reads these lines is old enough in years, understanding enough in mind to know that there are some uses of speech to which God never expected Christians to give themselves. Gossip, unfair criticism, cursing, swearing, and vulgarity of any sort are uses to which the Christian's speech should never be put. Since the Christian knows better, he will do better in his speaking if he loves Christ to the point of wanting all of his life to be acceptable. Again we notice that we are asked to lay aside all *evil speaking*.

The cure for evil speaking must be accomplished in the individual's heart. If thoughts of evil and emotions of wrong are not tolerated in the Christian's mind and heart, there will be little likelihood that evil speaking will emanate from his lips. Therefore, every one of us can pray with daily appropriateness the prayer of Psalm 19:14: "Let the words of my mouth, and the meditation of my heart, be acceptable in thy sight, O Lord, my strength and my redeemer."

We ask ourselves again: Are there some habits in our lives which could be viewed with understanding and patience if we were in our first months of following Jesus but which are completely out of character now that we have belonged to him for long enough to grow up? May God give to us the desire and courage to lay aside not only all malice, all guile, hypocrisies, envies, and all evil speaking, but every other habit which is not complimentary to the length of time in which we have walked with Jesus.

"As newborn babes, desire the sincere milk of the word, that ye may grow thereby" (1 Peter 2:2).

Dear Father, forgive us our childish ways, for we are ashamed that we have not laid them aside sooner. Help us now to step forth from spiritual childhood into spiritual maturity, and do save us from a relapse! Amen.

Nine

Multiplication

"So the men sat down, in number about five thousand. And Jesus took the loaves; and when he had given thanks, he distributed to the disciples, and the disciples to them that were set down; and likewise of the fishes as much as they would." John 6:10–11.

THE LUNCH WAS NOT LARGE, JUST FIVE little loaves and two little fishes. Had the growing, vigorous boy eaten all of it unaided, he would not have been overfull. The crowd gathered about the great Teacher was tremendous: at least five thousand men. Many were far from home; many would not find food when they returned; all of them were hungry.

Looked at through the eyes of men, the situation was impossible. The lunch was so small, the crowd was so large, and the treasury of the disciples was so nearly empty that the only recourse was to send the crowds away. Looked at through the eyes of the Son of God, the situation was easy. A surrendered lunch, the plus-mark of the power of God, and there would be food for all. There was no question concerning the need for food. There was no question concerning Christ's ability to bring the power of God to bear upon the situation. But would the little boy surrender his lunch?

Whether through obedient faith or simple astonishment the little boy gave up his lunch, we do not know. We do know, however, that there was evidently no reluctance on his part to place his simple gift in the hands of Jesus. We know, further, that Christ brought the multiplying power of God to bear upon that lunch, and it was multiplied into such proportions that five thousand people were fed amply—and a dozen baskets of fragments were left over. Thus was revealed an abiding principle: the individual who wishes his life multiplied to the maximum must place his life completely in the hands of Jesus.

In his wonderful ministry Christ demonstrated that abiding principle so often. He was almost perpetually taking little things and limited people who had placed themselves in his hands and multiplying them to amazing proportions of usefulness.

In his teaching, Christ took the simplest illustrations, clothed them with God's power, and turned them into never-to-be-forgotten truths. He spoke of birds of the air, lilies of the field, lost sheep, lost coins, sowing, reaping. Common figures these were until multiplied through the power of his use of them. The greatest lesson ever taught concerning humility was the lesson he taught with no more equipment than a basin and towel.

To perform some of his best remembered miracles, Christ had such simple materials: clay made of spittle, common water and urns, ordinary loaves and fishes, and a cross of wood so ignominious in that day that it carried an implication of sordid crime. He didn't have to have anything more than the simplest materials to perform the greatest miracles, provided those simple materials were placed with surrender in his hands.

He multiplied into world figures some people who, in the world's eyes, were "ignorant and unlearned." Peter and others were unknown fishermen whom the world would never have picked as powerful leaders for a spiritual movement. These simplest of people, placing themselves in the hands of Jesus, as surrendered as the loaves and fishes, were multiplied into a magnificent maximum of usefulness.

It is an abiding truth that every normal person wishes his life to amount to its maximum of usefulness and happiness. This desire of the human heart finds in the abiding principle of the loaves and fishes its only hope of fulfilment. No life can be multiplied to its maximum in any other way than by depositing itself in full surrender in the hands of Jesus. For each of three groups of people this principle carries a special message: warning for one, hope for another, and a lift for the third.

I

This principle of multiplication carries a warning to the brilliant and gifted ones. Though these gifted ones may achieve much of success and fame without depositing themselves in the hands of Jesus, they can never arrive at God's maximum of success for their lives in any other way. They may do much and even more, but they will never find the most of either success or happiness. They may experience for themselves and give to their world much of the good, even the better, but never the best unless they themselves are, like the lad's loaves and fishes, placed in full surrender in the hands of Jesus.

The rich young ruler may have made his mistake at this point. Without placing himself in the hands of Jesus in either faith or surrender, he had achieved remarkable success. When he counted the cost of making right the one thing which he lacked, it is possible that he concluded that he could achieve his maximum without that surrender. What did this brilliant, promising one achieve of lasting fame by ignoring this principle of multiplication to the maximum? Nothing for which the world remembers him! What did he lose? The possibility of usefulness in the fellowship of Christ.

When Paul proceeded upon the Damascus road that day, he was one of the most brilliantly prepared young men of his day. He was in the highest esteem in Jewish circles. His future was nothing short of scintillating in its promise. In the remarkable experience which came to him before that journey was finished, he followed the wise example of the lad with the loaves and fishes. The multiplying force of the power of God as a result of that surrender brought Paul to immortality of success and influence.

The pages of Christian history are liberally dotted with the record of gifted people who came to be of maximum success and usefulness while they lived and of immortal influence beyond their deaths because of this same principle of surrender. The late Mr. Kraft and the late Mr. Colgate—men whose names stand at the very top of the roster of business and industrial success in America—were not only devout Christians; they regarded themselves as servants through whom Jesus, into whose hands they had placed themselves like loaves and fishes, had the prior privilege of working to accomplish God's maximum purpose for their lives. They not only achieved maximum success in their respective fields of manufacturing; they achieved, also, such spiritual significance that their names will be associated always with the idea of dedicated Christian laymen.

Dr. Wilfred Grenfell, brilliant and successful doctor in one of London's elite sections, capable of achieving national and international fame in the field of medicine, placed himself completely in the hands of Jesus. The result of that act sent him to the barren wastes of Labrador to minister in the spirit of Christ to the privation-bound people there. One indication of the significance of his work is that he was knighted by the king of England. Sir Wilfred Grenfell will be remembered and honored forever with the world's truly great men. Gifted though he was in his own abilities, he was multiplied, like Paul, to dimensions which otherwise he would never have reached.

There are gifted men and women in all the vocations in our world today who testify eagerly that their "going all the way with Jesus" has brought power and achievement which could never have come otherwise. That sort of surrender in a doctor's life, for instance, will add a priceless plus which will make of him a better doctor and which will make of his life a greater contribution to medicine. The abiding principle of multiplication to the maximum through a self-surrender to the hands of Jesus has been neither amended nor revoked!

II

In the cold materialism of the business world, broken vessels are either discarded outright or are sold at greatly reduced prices. But when Jesus looks upon the broken vessels of human life, he neither discards them nor discounts them. On the contrary, he has so magnificently used the maimed and handicapped ones through the centuries as conveyers of strength and inspiration. No finer demonstration of his love and power to multiply can be found than in the lives of "broken vessels" completely surrendered and marvelously used!

Far from feeling despair, the handicapped Christian can rejoice in the knowledge that his usefulness can actually be multiplied because of his handicap. When the Christian places himself completely in the multiplying hands of Jesus, blindness becomes a blessing, lameness becomes a source of strength, limitations of any sort from any source are turned into assets.

Our very weaknesses and even our mistakes of the past, when deposited in his hands, are turned into strength and wisdom. Though our lives have been virtually broken to pieces by tragedy, he can put the pieces together into a mosaic which, as a masterpiece, will inspire the world. There is no handicapped person who cannot be multiplied into the maximum of usefulness, but the cost of the multiplication is the placing of one's self with faith and surrender in the hands of Jesus.

A wonderful young woman in Virginia has been confined to an iron lung for more than seven years. Handicapped? The world generally might say "Yes"; but this magnificent Christian has turned even an iron lung into a medium of maximum service. She dispenses more cheer, more genuine inspiration, and more vital help to people who need courage for their difficulties than any other person in her entire area. The secret? She would tell you gladly and quickly, if you had not already sensed it in your first five minutes with her, that Christ is the answer.

Handicapped? Think for a moment of Helen Keller, almost incomparable and surely immortal in the ranks of those who have triumphed over seemingly insurmountable handicaps. Originally bereft of the powers of hearing, speech, and sight, she linked her own magnificent determination with the power of God and with the help of a devoted teacher. The result has been such a triumph that there are people who almost envy her handicaps!

Handicapped by an unfortunate past? Think of Paul's pre-conversion record, of the woman at the well of Sychar! Handicapped by limited education? Think of Dwight L. Moody, or of William Carey, who had far less of formal education than even most preachers and missionaries of their day. Handicapped by *anything?* Remember and believe Philippians 4:13!

III

There is no finer demonstration of the goodness and love of God than in this principle of multiplication-to-maximum by depositing one's life in the hands of Christ, for through this principle even the one-talented person is assured of usefulness beyond any dimensions he could achieve alone. Those who do the simple, unheralded duties of life, those whose largest contribution to church is a radiant faithfulness in attendance, those who feel themselves to be the tiniest pebbles on the beach of life may well be thrilled by the realization that God has provided a principle by which their little efforts can be multiplied like loaves and fishes into blessings for many people.

The poor widow's mites would have gone unnoticed and unpraised in the world's scale of values. Jesus multiplied her wee gift into a superlatively large inspiration for all ages. As long as the world stands, that little woman's gift will be an example which challenges. Mary and Martha, whose gift was one of simple hospitality to Jesus, would not have been mentioned in the press notices of our day since their gift was so ordinary. To Jesus, however, that gift was important. Through his own attitude toward the contribution of Mary and Martha, Jesus multiplied their usefulness-through-example into immortality. And we continue to remember with joy the insignificant little lad with his loaves and fishes!

In the spring of 1953, an aged news vendor in a Southern city gave up his work after decades of faithful, radiant service in his little niche of life. On the day of his departure to live with relatives in the East, the large afternoon paper of his city contained his picture and an editorial eulogy of some length, conferring upon him the title "Mr. Inspiration." The spirit of Christ within his heart had multiplied this man, little and humble as the world counts greatness, into a personality and into an influence which blessed a city.

An elevator operator of limited education and restricted abilities placed herself so completely in the hands of Jesus that his wonderful spirit possessed her. In the busy building in which she operated an elevator, there were scores of the city's most gifted professional men and their talented employees who loved and respected her, and who sought her out when their own spirits needed the lift which only implicit Christian faith can bring.

A Negro janitor of meager capacities but of tremendous devotion to Christ and to the college for which he worked, made a contribution so large that the students have preserved his name and significance for posterity through an impressive bronze tablet.

"The stone which the builders refused is become the head stone of the corner" (Psalm 118:22) has been re-enacted many times in the history of Christianity. Little people, whom the world has ignored, undervalued, or rejected in choosing its leaders, have been multiplied to immortality by the abiding principle of placing themselves completely in the hands of Jesus. It has turned out that in almost every community some of the greatest sources of inspiration are little-talented people or people of exceedingly humble position who have placed every crumb of their lives in the Master's hands. Their radiant faith, their heart-warming humility, their complete devotion to Christ, and their joyous giving of their utmost in Christian service bless their communities immeasurably more than the lives of the more gifted ones who are not completely in the hands of Jesus.

On the basis of the amount of your life which is now completely controlled by Christ, what are the possibilities of your being multiplied to God's maximum intention for your life?

Heavenly Father, forgive us for the selfishness and vanity with which we have sought to multiply our own lives to selfish ends. Help us to be wise enough to act upon the knowledge that only in the hands of Jesus can any of us ever amount to thy best for us. Amen.

Ten

Punctuation

"Ye are our epistle written in our hearts, known and read of all men."
2 Corinthians 3:2.

$\mathbf{P}$AUL'S REMINDER THAT THE INDIVIDUAL'S life is a living epistle is a clever and dynamic figure. It follows logically that the living epistle, like written epistles, is being read by many people every day. These readers read some things from the epistle and some things *into* the epistle, and they do much of their reading when the individual is least conscious of the fact that his life is being read at all.

An epistle generally brings a message from one person to another. It is important, therefore, that the message intended by the writer shall be conveyed clearly to the reader. Any factor which causes the message to be misread, misinterpreted, or misunderstood is deplorable. One of the factors which can interfere with the proper reading and understanding of an epistle or essay is the factor of punctuation.

In the years of my teaching freshman English in college, I had a perpetual struggle to persuade the students of the "puddin' head" sections that punctuation is a necessity, not a luxury. Many of the students in those sections had the feeling that punctuation at the end of a sentence was adequate; or, in a moment of generosity, they would toss in a few commas with no clear concept of where or why. My first objective, therefore, was to convince the students that punctuation is imperative to a clear presentation of one's ideas.

To clinch my arguments in this connection, I brought to the classes many news clippings and printed illustrations which re-enforced the argument that punctuation can make a major difference in the meaning of a group of words or even in the legal interpretation of a document. Two true life instances follow.

A secretary, who had brought suit against a former employer for dismissing her for the simple omission of "one little old comma" from a document, lost her suit in the courts. The presentation of the document by the defendant revealed that the omission of that comma had rendered the text liable to misreading and misinterpretation, and that the company had lost $50,-000 as a result of the omission of that "one little old comma."

Our nation lost in one year a million dollars of import taxes which the Congress in the late 1860's had intended. In grouping the commodities for varying rates of import taxation, the committee had separated the groups by semicolons, the amount of tax to be indicated by the group in which each commodity stood. Therefore, it mattered on which side of the semicolon a commodity was placed. A misplaced semicolon in this instance placed a group of commodities in a lower bracket of taxation than had been intended. The government thereby lost a million dollars of anticipated revenue before the next session of Congress could correct the punctuation of the law.

To illustrate to the still unconvinced student that a mark or two of punctuation can change completely the meaning of a sentence, I commandeered a very old illustration: "Woman without her man would go insane." With only the period at the end of the sentence, the meaning is clear: the woman goes insane. The insertion of two simple marks of punctuation can change the meaning of that sentence completely. To illustrate: "Woman: without her, man would go insane."

The analogy is clear: If written epistles can be misread so that their intended messages are either misunderstood or not clearly conveyed because the punctuation is inadequate or inaccurate, these living epistles can, also, fail to convey their finest and highest messages—not because our intentions are not good, but because of the omission of some matters which are as important to good Christian living as punctuation is essential to good writing.

In my teaching experiences, it was always a source of regret to me to have to give an essay a grade lower than the quality of the content justified, just because the necessary punctuation was omitted. It must be a source of poignant regret to the great Teacher to observe that our living epistles are failing to score the significance which the hope of his heart and ours aspires to, just because of some equally significant omissions. In the spirit of the analogy, let's take a look at a few marks of punctuation.

I

In the scheme of punctuation there are marks which are called "pause marks." These are marks which will indicate to the wise reader the length of pause and the amount of drop in the voice expected at that point. The comma indicates the shortest pause; the period indicates the longest and most complete pause. The wise placing of these pause marks will make the reader's task immeasurably easier and his joy in reading a passage much keener. They add an expressiveness of spirit and manner which would be lacking otherwise.

There are times in the Christian's life in which pauses are of great significance, and the failure to pause at these times and for the proper length of time can make of his living epistle a less effective message than it would be otherwise. Here are some times of important pause.

The Christian ought to pause to pray. Prayer is both a period and a comma. It is a period in that there should be a definite time in the course of the day in which the Christian stops completely everything else in his life and occupies himself exclusively with a heart-impelled communication with God. Prayer is a comma, too, in that the Christian should lift little moments and petitions of prayer from time to time throughout the day as new impulses and needs arise.

The Christian ought to pause to read God's Word.
This pause to read God's Word is as essential to victorious living as the pause to look at a road map is important to successful traveling in unfamiliar areas. The Bible is the all-sufficient guide to human conduct. Without its guidance the Christian submits himself to the possibility of getting off onto some wrong roads, unnecessary detours, and avoidable doubts and defeats. The daily pause to read God's Word is a pause which reveals, illumines, and empowers.

The Christian needs an occasional "inventory pause." If it is good business in the commercial world to make a periodic pause for inventory, it is good business to make a similar pause to examine our spiritual condition. In the first place, this pause enables the Christian to check up on his spiritual growth with such questions as these. Am I growing in strength in my prayer life, in my hold upon God's Word, in faith, in conviction? Is my compassion for the spiritual needs of others growing and demonstrating itself in more personal effort at soul winning? Am I serving more readily in keeping with my capacities? Am I developing more comprehensively the Christian virtues of patience, sympathy, understanding, forgiveness, humility, unselfishness, and long-suffering love?

In the second place, this inventory pause should occur in every instance in which the Christian senses a loss of power, peace, or joy in his life. In the pause the Christian will do well to ask himself some of the following questions. Has a sin come into my life, separating me from a closeness to Jesus? Have I been failing to do the things which bring power and joy into the Christian's life? Have I neglected to put first things first in my life? In this inventory pause the Christian can find the cause for any loss of spiritual fitness!

The Christian should pause frequently to help other people. There are so many fellow pilgrims around us who have loads which we can lift or which we can carry for them for a while. There are those about us whose problems we can help to solve, whose questions we can help to answer, whose sorrows we can share, whose doubts we can dispel, whose confusions we can clarify, whose defeats we can soften.

To pause to whisper a word of cheer to someone who lacks courage, to pause to do a courteous act, to pause to drop a bit of inspiration into someone's erstwhile drab life amounts to releasing fragrance into other people's lives. A practical philosopher pointed out one time that the dispenser of perfume will always catch some of the fragrance in his own clothes and hair.

Though the Christian who pauses to help others should be motivated only by the desire to do the Christlike and Christ-honoring service, an inspiring consequence of this kind of pausing is that, when this Christian's turn comes to drink of the bitter cup, all the pausing which he has done to help others will come back to him, multiplied and with interest paid.

For eighteen years following my graduation from college I had been busy in my work, much of which had to do with pausing to counsel and to help other people. Then, with great suddenness, in June of 1947 my own turn came to taste the cup of suffering. In an automobile accident, I was critically injured. For ten weeks I was confined to a traction bed in a hospital, and for several months thereafter I was abed in a cast.

During those eventful weeks of hospitalization, I was overwhelmed by the truth that all of one's pausing to help others does come back to him in his hour of need. Five thousand people wrote letters of sympathy and good wishes; four hundred and fifty people sent telegrams; nearly five hundred sent gifts of various sorts to cheer me; enough flowers came to stock a huge flower shop; so many hundreds of friends called upon me that I was in a constant state of reunion! All my remaining years, I shall value the pause marks of life.

II

Usage has confined the *question mark* to two principal uses: at the end of a group of words which ask a question, and in parentheses after a date or statement to indicate that there is doubt in the writer's mind concerning the accuracy of the information just given. In these living epistles the question mark arises normally in these two instances, too.

The question mark which seeks information should appear in the Christian's life generously and constantly. The hunger to *know* more of the sources of spiritual power and to experience them, the search for more of truth as revealed in God's Word, and the eagerness to know human needs and to relate them to

God's power should impel the Christian to a life-long quest. When the Christian ceases to want new information concerning the spiritual implications of life, he has ceased to use the question mark in his living epistle. Stagnation of life will ensue inevitably, for the Christian who ceases to learn will surely cease to grow.

The question mark enclosed in parentheses indicates doubt, but the good scholar will not be satisfied to leave the doubt there. Through research and consultation he will seek to remove the doubt, to replace the question mark with the period, indicating that fact has replaced uncertainty. The coming of doubts into the Christian's life is normal. The doubts may even indicate that he is searching for fuller truth.

There came honest doubts into the minds of Nathanael (John 1:46), John the Baptist (Luke 7:19), and Thomas (John 20:24–28). In these three instances the doubts were dispelled as all doubts in the Christian's life can be dispelled. Each made new, fresh, intimate contact with Jesus, and the doubts disappeared. As quickly as doubt comes into his heart, the Christian should weigh the doubt in fervent periods of prayer and Bible study. If the doubt persists, he will be wise to take it to a trusted friend whose objective view and greater wisdom will often chart the way out of the confusion of doubt.

III

As we know, the chief use of the *quotation marks* is to enclose a direct quotation, normally indicating that the material enclosed is not that of the writer, but that it has been borrowed from someone else to enforce the writer's point of view. Therefore, these quotation marks become a badge of honesty, proclaiming to all who read that the principle of honesty has been observed.

In our day, this badge of honesty is urgently needed in the Christian's life. Dishonesty has come to be so widespread that Christian students are frequently involved in cheating, Christian business and professional men are involved in illegal maneuverings, some Christians who hold offices of public trust are found to be dishonest. Christianity and honesty ought to be synonymous in the minds of people, so that anyone could reply with certainty, "Of course he doesn't cheat; he is a Christian."

Honesty in thinking, speaking, appraising, and acting will structure an individual's life with steel beams of strength. Insincerity, exaggeration, duplicity of any sort will damage the very foundation of character. The Christian may well pray that God will give to him unusual perception and power to withstand the increasingly widespread and socially acceptable practices of hypocrisy. There are no more refreshing, stimulating, inspiring marks of punctuation than the quotation marks!

A teacher had stood her turn in the long line at the post-office stamp window. When her purchase was completed and she was walking away, she suspected from the amount of silver given her by the stamp salesman that she had received too much change. She rechecked the cost of the stamps, counted the change, and discovered that she had received seventy-nine cents too much from the salesman. She took her place again in the line to await another turn at the window. When she showed the figures to the salesman and returned the change, he smiled with surprise and said with admiration: "Folks like you are surely rare. Say, you must be a Christian!" The quotation marks were conspicuous in her living epistle.

IV

As we remember from our grade school days, the *exclamation point* indicates sudden or strong feeling on the part of the writer or speaker and should be reserved for use with expressions which contain genuine warmth or excitement or emphasis. An overuse of the exclamation point will inevitably diminish its effectiveness, because the reader will cease to be alerted by its appearance.

In these living epistles, the exclamation point does have a place; and, as in the written epistle, it should be used wisely and appropriately. In the Christian's experiences, there are times in which he ought to be indignant, in which he ought to speak up with the warmth of conviction to defend principles, in which he ought to speak with emotion and compassion. Wanting these times to mean what they ought to mean in spiritual impact, however, the Christian will make sure that the time of vigorous speaking is justified by the principles involved.

V

The *capital letter* is, in a special way, a mark of punctuation. The use of the capital letter in the body of the sentence indicates a proper name or a proper noun. Its correct use indicates, further, that the writer of the sentence has a sense of values which distinguishes between the common and proper nouns. The unknowing writer will capitalize the common and commonize the proper, revealing a basic ignorance or carelessness or disrespect.

To make his living epistle of maximum significance, the Christian, too, needs to develop a sense of values which will enable him to discern the matters and principles of life which are the more important. To these more important matters, he will give more time, energy, and devotion. To the lesser values, he will logically give lesser significance. To the principles which are of greater importance, he will give the greater deference and respect.

This sense of values will result in the Christian's capitalizing the names and persons of God, Christ, and Holy Spirit. He will capitalize through greater deference and practice such matters as Bible study, prayer, faith, surrender, purity, sacrifice, service, honor, humility, kindness, love, and forgiveness. To the reading world, the Christian's living epistle will portray in the very honor and emphasis placed upon these matters his own sense of values, leading some of the readers logically to an acceptance of the same values.

A final challenge to writers of living epistles is this: *learn to do your own punctuating.* Don't depend upon other people, even those who love you most, to carry the responsibility for telling you when to pause and for how long, to find the answers for all of your questions, to determine when the quotation marks are in order, to call for an exclamation point or to cancel one, or to tell you what to capitalize. It is a reflection upon the adequacy of an individual's education or upon his spiritual insight if he must depend upon others to give directions for punctuating his essay.

Do you remember the classic episode of the student who wrote his essay with little or no punctuation and who "heaped" all the various marks up at the end of the paper with this notation: "Dear Teacher: here they are; please put them in where they're needed"? The teacher's disgust, if not despair can be imagined. The student's grade, despite whatever excellence the content of his paper may have had, can be predicted. Punctuation matters!

Our Teacher and Lord, place in our hearts an extra spark of spiritual ambition, that we may aspire to be right not only in our intentions, but, also, in the manner in which these intentions are conveyed to our world. Help us to be wise enough to know that punctuation is important, whether the epistle be written or lived. Amen.

Eleven

The Four M's

"And if I bestow all my goods to feed the poor, and if I give my body to be burned, but have not love, it profiteth me nothing." 1 Corinthians 13:3 ASV.

THE WORD "SERVICE" ROLLS SO EASILY down our tongues and out our lips. In fact, its use has come to be so broad and so shallow that its poignant meaning in application to genuine service is almost lost to many of us. We are inclined to speak of any meeting of religious nature as "service," or we allude to the performance of almost any little chore related to our church lives as an act of service. Almost anything (or nothing!) is "service" in the average Christian's terminology!

Since no Christian can grow into spiritual maturity unless his life is becoming increasingly a medium for spiritual service, it is important that we examine our so-called service activities in the light of some principles which will X-ray these activities to ascertain whether or not they constitute genuine Christian service. We need to try to recapture for our guidance the vital spiritual significance of the word "service." For clear analysis and easy remembering, let's speak of the four M's of Christian service.

I

M for "Meaning." What does Christian service actually mean? Perhaps we can begin best by tabulating some things it is not. It is not merely attending meetings. Though some individuals do perform service in connection with meetings of church nature, for most of us who attend, these meetings are more nearly banquets which serve us bountiful spiritual food. It would be little short of absurd for a guest to say, after eating a generous meal, "I have rendered a fine service to my hostess."

It is not paying for our salvation on the installment plan! Ephesians 2:8-9 has made convincingly clear the impossibility of earning salvation: "For by grace are ye saved through faith; and that not of yourselves: it is the gift of God: not of works, lest any man should boast." Yet a surprisingly large number of Christians, when asked to continue serving or to take additional responsibilities in keeping with their abilities, reply in terms which leave the impression that they have just about "squared" things with the Lord, that their obligations to him are almost "paid up."

It may seem redundant for this to be said, but it is of surpassing importance that every Christian of us remember that when we have fulfilled all that duty suggests, we are still unworthy servants; that if we should serve to the limit of our abilities to the limit of our days, we shall not have done enough to make a "down payment" on the priceless gift of our salvation.

Christian service is not a scheme for atoning for past sins, nor for achieving favor with God for future requests. Offhand, it would seem unnecessary to offer this reminder to Christians; yet, many who have been active in church life assume attitudes when losses come or when requests of their hearts are not granted which amount to their saying, "Why should this happen to me after all I've done for the Lord?"

What, then, is Christian service? Put in its simplest terms, Christian service is the Christian's fulfilment of the request of Christ in John 21:15–17, ". . . Lovest thou me? . . . Feed my sheep." The true meaning of Christian service is found, therefore, in the Christian's rendering every service possible in keeping with his capacities and opportunities, rendering this service as a proof positive of his love for Jesus.

What happens to a mother's heart when her little daughter runs in from the yard with a hand full of flowers, giving them radiantly to her mother with the words, "I brought them 'cause I love you so much"? Or when a little son brings home from school his masterpiece of handwork with the declaration, "It's yours, Mom, 'cause the teacher told us to bring it to the person we love best"? In telling her friends of those episodes, the mother probably has difficulty restraining the tears as she says, "Bless their little hearts. If they never do anything else for me, I shall feel compensated in those precious little deeds!"

Had those children paid back their mother for all of her service, suffering, and sacrifice in their behalf? No. Yet, they had given to the person who made possible their birth and happiness a token which revealed love and gratitude. Though the Christian can never "pay back" his Lord through even limitless service, he can be saying perpetually, "Lord, though I can never be worthy of your death in my behalf, and though I can never compensate you for a gift so large as eternal life, I can keep feeding your sheep . . . I can keep on saying in these tangible ways that my love for you is deep and growing."

II

M for "Motive." In the truest analysis, the motive with which the Christian renders his service will determine whether or not it is service which just anybody can render or whether it is Christian service, which only the Christian can render and which is the only kind of service that is acceptable to our Lord.

It is true that many Christians serve with wrong or lesser or inadequate motives. In serving with such motives, the Christian not only fails to please Jesus, but he fails, also, to experience in his service-life the true joy which genuine Christian service always brings. Let us take a quick look at some of these unacceptable motives.

Duty impels many Christians to serve. Duty is surely not an unworthy motive, but it is not the highest motive, nor is it an adequate motive. If duty is the determining motive of an individual's life, he will serve un-til he feels that he has fulfilled his duty but will feel no obligation to go beyond that point. Duty will take us far along the road of acceptable service, but duty alone will never take us far enough, surely not to the maxi-mum point.

Reciprocation as a motive is not bad; yet it is even less adequate than a sense of duty as a motivation. Re-ciprocation will mean that we shall feel that we have served adequately when we have repaid all the favors done for us or all the services accorded us. This motive is not only inadequate; it can be, also, quite selfish. Can you imagine Christ's simply reciprocating the few and paltry favors done for him?

Love for people, though essential to acceptable Christian service, is not of itself an adequate motive. Many people who work in the field of human relations love to be with people, enjoying their fellowship, en-joying the compensating privilege of doing favors for them. This kind of love can be an ego-inflating experi-ence and not necessarily anchored to the greater achievement of loving people for Jesus' sake. If the Christian does not love Jesus first of all and most of all, and if he does not love people through the heart of Jesus and for Jesus' sake, his love for people will mean that he will serve only those who appeal to him or only so long as serving people appeals to him. It can be, therefore, both inadequate and unworthy as a motiva-tion for Christian service.

Thrill in performing, stimulation in persuading

people, enjoyment of praise following service are manifestly unworthy as motives for Christian service. Though it is thoroughly normal for an individual to appreciate praise, for instance, that enjoyment should be so incidental and unnecessary to his service-life that he will continue to serve in the total absence of praise just as fully and joyously. Here, as in the other motives listed above, the Christian needs a higher, more adequate motivation.

What, then, is the adequate motive for Christian service? It is presented with unmistakable clarity and glorious warmth in 1 Corinthians 13. Put in its clearest terms, that adequate motivation is *personal love for Jesus Christ.* If I love him with all my heart, serving him will be an imperative urge and an unremitting joy. Regardless of the quantity of my service, if this determining motive is not present in my heart, the service is not acceptable to Christ. "If I speak with the tongues of men and of angels, but have not love, I am become sounding brass, or a clanging cymbal . . . And if I give my body to be burned, but have not love, it profiteth me nothing" (1 Cor. 13:1, 3 ASV).

It is evident, therefore, that a Christian could teach a Sunday school class or function as a leader in any capacity or many capacities for twenty-five years without actually performing any acceptable Christian service—all because he was not impelled in his service by a personal love for Jesus Christ.

Are you doing that job or those jobs with the right motive? If no one ever praised or appreciated or reciprocated, would you keep on doing just what you are now doing and with deep gratification for the privilege of doing the service for Jesus' sake? If somebody were unkind to you or critical of your work or even basely unworthy of your efforts, would you find in your love for Jesus Christ sufficient motivation to keep on serving?

We sat at the conclusion of a truly clever "sweetheart banquet" in which the decorations, program, and food had vied with each other in their superlative excellence. Some people had worked hard, very hard, to make that banquet a glorious experience. The toastmaster thanked a round of people with appropriate eulogies, but he overlooked inadvertently the lady who had done most of the food preparation! Though the oversight was deplorable, it was surely not deliberate.

The benediction had been pronounced, and almost everyone had departed. I stood in conversation with friends who were waiting for candlesticks to be gathered. Out of the kitchen came the overlooked lady. She was indignant almost to the point of volcanic explosion.

"They can just eat paper napkins up here from now on out, so far as I am concerned," she declared. "I came up here early this morning, worked my fingers to the bone nearly all day, and do you think that the toastmaster even so much as thanked me publicly? Indeed, he did not!" And she proceeded to whisk articles off the table with evident venom.

As deplorable as was the toastmaster's oversight,

more deplorable was this Christian woman's display of a selfish motivation for Christian service. It was evident that in her all-day toil in the kitchen, she had been imagining a scene at the end of the banquet: She would be called out of the kitchen; she would go, reluctantly, of course; and, as she stood in the limelight, the toast-master would exhaust his supply of superlatives in eulogizing her; and, midst gales of applause, she would bow back to the kitchen in a blaze of glory! Though she had worked all day in a so-called Christian service, she had rendered no acceptable service. She was serving, not primarily for Jesus' sake, but because of her own selfish desires for praise and publicity.

III

M for "Measure." What measuring stick can I use to make sure that I am rendering all the service which I ought to render? The very best measuring rod for the Christian's use is found in Acts 3:6. Peter, not having money to give to the beggar at the Temple gate, said to him, "Silver and gold have I none; but such as I have give I thee." This principle, applied to the Christian's service-life, means that he will, on the one hand, not worry that he cannot do some things in service which others can do, and that he will, on the other hand, do with gladness what he can do—and everything that he can do.

Apply that measuring stick to your service-life. If you are one of God's five-talented children, are you using all five of those talents in Christian service? If your talents number four, three, two, or just one, are you so completely using every one of them that you can look up into his face with truth and joy to say, "Lord, such as I have in ability to serve I am giving back to you gladly in Christian service"? In the light of the parable of talents in Matthew 25:14–30, would you be entitled today to receive his "Well done, good and faithful servant"?

One of the most inspiring memories in my heart is the memory of an underprivileged lad in one of the churches in which I filled an appointment. There was great pathos in his appearance. He was noticeably wan in physical strength, and his clothes were both ill-fitting and inadequate for the severe weather which prevailed. His faithfulness in attending the meetings and his rapt attention in every moment of the messages had touched my heart deeply.

This lad was clearly depressed on the night in which offering envelopes were made available, because he had nothing to give. When he gave such evidence of sorrow that he could not make a financial contribution to the meetings, I wished that it were possible for me to sit alongside him to say, "O little boy, God doesn't expect you to give money. He knows that you have neither silver nor gold to give. But he knows, as I surely know, that you have given to me the finest inspiration of the week in your coming despite obvious hunger and inadequate clothing. Such as you have, you have given, and the gift is magnificent."

Though I had feared that he might not return for

the closing night, he was present. Furthermore, he no longer looked depressed, even when the offering plates were passed. As I stood after the benediction to bid good-by to many people, this little lad pressed up to me, placed in my hands a folded piece of simple pencil-tablet paper, and said timidly, "Don't look at this 'till you get out of town." With that, he darted out of the church and into the night.

When the train on which I was departing had passed beyond the city limits, I slipped out the little piece of paper, unfolded it, and looked at it with unusual interest. On it the lad had drawn a simple cottage with trees and walkway. Underneath the picture, in awkward printing, done in his own inexperienced hand, were the cherished words: "I have drawn this picture for Mr. Swor, because I love him."

I made no attempt to restrain the tears which sprang up from a heart which remembered with stirring emotion Peter's wonderful words to the man at the Temple gate: "Silver and gold have I none; but such as I have give I thee." I felt that Christ himself would feel that this bit of paper was the most significant gift given that week. The lad, like the widow with her mites, had so wonderfully done what he could. He had surely achieved service to the proper measure!

IV

M for "Maximum." Service, when rendered to the maximum degree, always eventuates in sacrifice, for sacrifice is the logical culmination of genuine Christian

144

service. Many of us are as confused in our concepts of
sacrifice as we are in our concepts of service. Actually,
what is sacrifice?

Sacrifice is not a mere sharing of our plenty, nor is it
merely a giving up of some things in order to serve. During World War II some college girls announced that
they were "sacrificing" nylon hose for the remainder
of the war in order that the money saved could go into
Chinese relief. Girls on another campus announced
that they were "sacrificing" desserts in the dining hall
for the remainder of the session in behalf of the same
relief funds.

I laughed quietly in reading these news dispatches,
for they were indicative of the shallow concept of sacrifice in the heart of the average Christian in our land.
In giving up hose and desserts the college girls had
actually given up luxuries, or, in the most generous
interpretation, they had merely shared. They had not
sacrificed. Had they decided to give up the purchase of
all new clothes for the remainder of the war, or had
they decided to give up one full meal each day, a closer
approach to the true spirit of sacrifice would have been
made.

The beloved Mrs. J. M. Dawson once told a student
group a definition of sacrifice given by a child in a
group which she was addressing. The child's remarkable definition of sacrifice was this: "Sacrifice is giving up something you can't do without." Though no
dictionary will ever carry that definition, it is clearly
a magnificent one. The doing or giving when the act

involves some cost or hurt of genuine significance is the essence of sacrifice. Service to that degree emulates the spirit of Christ in giving up his residence in heaven to come for the sacrificial earthly ministry, and his spirit in giving up his life to make possible our reconciliation to God.

Have you ever relinquished something which you very much wanted, just because you felt that the desired something would impair your service-life? Have you ever given up a trip which you really wanted, just because you felt that remaining at home to fill your post of service was of greater importance? Have you ever given up anything, the giving up of which cost and hurt keenly, just for the sake of serving Christ more fully? Have you ever swallowed false pride and kept on serving? Have you kept on serving without a martyr complex when you were tired enough to drop in your tracks? If we haven't sacrificed in service, we have never reached the maximum of service; and if we have never served at the cost of sacrifice, we have missed the highest thrill of Christian service!

The meaning, the motive, the measure, and the maximum of service are clear. How does your service-life look now in the bright light of these principles and tests?

Generous, All-loving Father, do purge us of our selfishness in service. Help us, we pray, that we shall never again regard Christian service in the light and shallow ways in which most of us have regarded it heretofore.

Make us wise enough to know that we shall not only serve with more of ease, but with more of joy and to greater quantity when we are possessed of the wonderful motive, "For Jesus' sake." Amen.

Twelve

The Proof Supreme

"*Now when they saw the boldness of Peter and John, and perceived that they were unlearned and ignorant men, they marvelled; and they took knowledge of them, that they had been with Jesus.*" Acts 4:13.

IN THE FOURTH CHAPTER OF ACTS THERE IS the thrilling record of the appearance of Peter and John before a significant and menacing group of Jewish church officials. Peter, being the spokesman, replied to the inquiries and threats of the officials with eloquence and power which impressed even these antagonists of Christianity very greatly. Knowing that Peter and John had not come up through the channels of formal education, these leaders were hard pressed to explain their power and absolutely unable to "explain it away." Verse 13 contains a conclusion and a compliment: "Now when they saw the boldness of Peter and John, and perceived that they were unlearned and ignorant men, they marvelled; and they took knowledge of them, that they had been with Jesus."

Had these lofty officials of the Jewish church asked one of Peter's long-time associates about his experience, doubtless they would have received a thrilling report, which could have run somewhat as follows:

"If you could have known Peter as I knew him before he met this Christ, you would hardly recognize him as the same person now. Before he began to follow Christ, Peter had a vicious temper. His tongue was sharp and much feared in his community. He was vain, arrogant, self-centered. His great passion was to catch more fish than any other fisherman in his company.

"Then, one day, Peter met this strange man called Jesus, and the change in his life was almost incredible. The change has continued, growing more possessive of his personality until today I recognize only his physical appearance as being similar to his old self, and even that has lost its hardness. His strong temper, now controlled with a strange new power, is harnessed to a passionate preaching. His facile tongue delivers messages which are amazing. His arrogance, vanity, and self-centeredness are now replaced with humility, earnestness, and a consuming desire to win believers to his Christ. As I said, if I did not recognize his physical features, I couldn't believe that he is the Simon Peter whom I once knew. The change is amazing!"

Peter was not the only person of that day whose following Jesus made a transforming difference in the follower's life. Zaccheus, once a hated business-cheat, became a "second-mile" Christian businessman. The woman caught in the act of adultery became a woman of strength and a devout follower of Jesus. The woman at the well outside Sychar, married five times and then living as a social outcast with a man who was not her husband, met Jesus at the well and went back into her city redeemed and witnessing. Saul started down the Damascus road as one of Christianity's fiercest antagonists. He met Jesus in a memorable experience before that journey was complete, and he went on his way as Paul, one of Christianity's strongest defenders.

Down through the centuries of Christianity's history, the experience of transformation through contact with Jesus has been multiplied millions of times. People have met Jesus, have permitted him to possess their lives, and have become so wonderfully different that other people have marveled, and have taken knowledge that they have been with Jesus.

In fact, that is obviously the way Jesus intended Christianity to proceed: that an individual would be so changed that he would go on his way helping to change other lives, lives of people who would be more eager for the change within them because of what they had seen in the lives of those who had been with Jesus.

The greatest achievement of Christianity is what it does in the life of an individual. The only justifiable hope for the future of our world is that Christianity will be permitted to change enough lives to make a difference in the whole world, for a changed world surely depends upon changed people.

I

When Jesus is permitted to come into the heart of an individual, he performs regeneration: The individual is born again; he becomes a new creature. When Jesus is permitted full control of the Christian's life, he performs transformation: The individual's character and conduct are brought into an inspiring conformity to the spirit and teachings of Christ. When any person experiences genuine regeneration and complete transformation, his associates cannot fail to take knowledge of him, that he has been with Jesus.

Therefore, the supreme test of the genuineness and effectiveness of an individual's Christianity in the eyes of the world is its ability to make him different in character and conduct. The world is justified in doubting that regeneration has occurred if it does not see transformation in the life of the Christian. These deductions are in order: (1) There must be some things in our lives which are simply inexplainable except in terms of our having been with Jesus. These differences should become more obvious and numerous the longer we follow Jesus. (2) The living, possessing presence of Christ in our lives should be so complete that strangers coming into contact with us will discern immediately that we have been with Jesus. Radiance, gentleness, kindness, patience, unselfishness, and love which reveal the spirit of Christ will make it unnecessary for us to wear labels and to carry banners proclaiming that we are Christians! Our telling people that we are Christians ought to be only a confirmation of what they had already felt and not information which they had not already deduced!

The greatest need of our America is to know Jesus. The best opportunity which our America has to know Jesus is to see him in the daily living of you and me and

154

Christians like us, who will permit Jesus to possess us so completely that all who touch our lives will take sure knowledge that we have been with Jesus. For every Christian there is this question of urgent significance: Does my life in its daily walk pass the supreme test?

II

In almost every conceivable situation in our America today there are some Christians whose lives present the proof supreme that they have been with Jesus. Enough Christians are living this proof to make possible our saying two things: (1) Regardless of the difficulty of the circumstances under which a Christian is obliged to live, he can, with God's constant help, so live that people will know that he has been with Jesus. (2) If the individual does so live, some difference will occur in the attitude of other people toward Jesus. It will be both helpful and inspiring to look at a fine group of people whose lives have given this proof supreme. Of the following people we may say, "These passed the test!"

Bobby was only nine years old when he became a Christian. His parents were not only not Christians, they were extremely worldly in their living. They took the announcement of Bobby's having become a Christian with the feeling that he had been submitted to some pressure in Sunday school and that this "emotional excitement" would be of short duration. But they were in for the greatest discovery of their lives!

Bobby's entire habit pattern changed. He began to

be motivated in his behavior by the question, "What would Jesus do in this instance?" He purchased a Bible and began a faithful reading of God's Word and a nightly time of fervent prayer. He began to show genuine concern for the spiritual condition of his parents. He urged that thanks be offered at mealtimes, even though neither of his parents had ever prayed in his hearing.

You have surely anticipated the result of Bobby's transformed living in his home circle. Upon overhearing his tearful praying in their behalf as they passed his room on their way to bed, they spent a sleepless night. Before dawn, conviction of sin had come into their hearts with overwhelming force. Soon after breakfast, a minister was called. Before noon, Bobby's parents had given their hearts to Jesus in a thrilling experience of repentance and faith. They had found an unanswerable argument in the life of their son, who was different because he had been with Jesus.

"Say, *Phil* surely is different in his attitude toward me since he became a Christian," said a younger brother of a high school senior. "Now he doesn't storm at me any more. He turns off the radio when I have a headache; and, recently, he stayed at home to do my chores because he thought that I hadn't had my share of recreation lately."

Phil's parents, themselves not Christians, are amazed by the improvement of his school grades now that he brings home some A's for the first time. They not only do not understand, but are evidently impatient that Phil is unwilling to buy any new clothes unless there is almost emergency need. With winsome humility, Phil simply explains that there are needs so much greater in the world and that he prefers to give almost all of his clothes allowance to missions. His whole motivation for the future now is Christ-centered. Whereas he formerly planned a brilliant career "for Phil's sake," now he is dedicated to medical missions "for Jesus' sake." Brother, parents, and a multitude of school friends are taking knowledge of Phil, that he has been with Jesus!

A vital and thrilling part of Phil's story is that he came to be a Christian because of the beautiful spirit of Christ which he saw in the life of a girl whom he dated and because of the equally wonderful Christian spirit which he recognized in her parents and in her home life. When one person's living indicates that he has been with Jesus, another takes knowledge, and another, and another . . . down through the days and the centuries!

Many people told me with anxious concern of a *teacher* in a select private school in a city in which I was speaking for a week. Though he had a most persuasive personality, he was an unfortunate influence in the school because of lax speech and frequent drunkenness. Furthermore, he was abusive in his home life when he was intoxicated. His widely beloved wife was among the Christians who prayed most urgently for him. The hope and prayer of many people and many years had a glorious reward in the man's coming forward in the services with genuine indication of having given his heart to Jesus.

After three years I returned to the same city. His name, his wonderful influence, and his devotion to Christ were the chief topics of conversation all over the little city. The school in which he taught had been almost completely transformed. His devoted wife told me that the last three years had been virtual "honeymoon years" because of his love and devotion. A whole city took knowledge that this man had been with Jesus!

As a result of the dedication of their lives to a more consistent living of Christian principles in their high school, *three girls* made such a difference that a teacher of twenty years' experience in that school told me this wonderful thing two years later: "Whereas the majority sentiment of this school was formerly so completely lax and loose that much vulgarity prevailed, the majority sentiment is now so motivated by the Christian spirit and principle that the whole school is being transformed."

Dan was president of his fraternity. Therefore, he presided at a dinner meeting which I attended in the fraternity house. The spirit of the entire evening had been as wholesome as the keenest Christian could hope for. Now that the dinner was concluded, greetings were expressed to the visitors. Thereafter, Dan suggested that the fraternity sing some of its favorite tunes. It was not surprising that two or three numbers of some historical connection with the fraternity were sung first. Then, as if it were as normal as eating, the fraternity sang some of the most spiritual of the youth choruses of our day.

I left that fraternity dinner meeting with these two impressions: that the atmosphere was almost that of a religious organization for students, and that the existence of such an atmosphere was neither "usual" nor accidental. I knew that somebody had lived with conviction, consecration, and courage to bring the atmosphere of a social fraternity to that point of excellence.

Upon inquiry I learned that Dan himself was responsible. During his first two years in the fraternity, Dan had so completely hidden the fact that he was a Christian that nobody would have suspected any allegiance on his part to Jesus. Then there was an experience which Dan interpreted as being nothing short of regeneration. Though the going in his fraternity thereafter was not easy, he won the fraternity to a better way of life through testimony, explanation, courage, humility, unselfishness, and long-suffering. In the first year after his own experience with Jesus, Dan won eight of his fraternity brothers to Christ. A whole fraternity took knowledge that Dan had been with Jesus; and the president of the college told me that the whole campus had taken knowledge of that fraternity, that it had been transformed!

Bill tended the soup section of the cafeteria in his college, a position in which he was subjected to all the quips of clever collegians concerning the content (or lack of content) of cafeteria soup. He had not only taken the job in stride, but had made that section of the cafeteria line into a high point of cheer for the passing throngs. His clever repartee first attracted me. Then I saw in his whole manner a magnetism which comes only when one has been with Jesus to the point of total surrender. When I sat down to dine with the director of religious life, I made inquiry of Bill's Christian experience. The story was thrilling.

Bill had had a campus-wide reputation for great proficiency in gambling. Though rumor had probably magnified his skill and his winnings, the rumor, shorn of exaggeration, left the fact that Bill was possessed by a fever for winning other people's possessions. In an experience almost as traumatic as that of Paul on the Damascus road, Bill came face to face with Jesus. The change in his life matched that in Paul's life in both suddenness and completeness. Before sunset on the day of his conversion, he had destroyed all of his gambling paraphernalia and was already talking to his gambling buddies in an attempt to lead them to Jesus.

The news of Bill's conversion stirred the campus deeply. The unmistakable transformation of his character and conduct thereafter proved to even the most cynical doubters that Bill's experience was genuine and abiding. The blasé critic could no longer say that Christianity was only for girls and preacher boys! The Christian student could no longer despair of even the most difficult unsaved student in the college. One boy had been with Jesus, and the whole campus took knowledge of the transformation. In my four nights of speaking in a nearby church, I, too, took knowledge that Bill had been with Jesus, for he brought seven fellow students down the aisles for professions of faith.

I had boarded a train in the midst of the worst of war-time train travel and had been directed to the only vacant seat in the car. The seat was alongside *a very old lady* who was on her way for summer in New England after a winter in Florida. Her radiant spirit in welcoming me to the seat, and her heart-warming spirit of concern for the happiness of the many soldiers in the car led me to an early impression that she had been with Jesus. Every passing minute deepened that impression. The soldiers had sensed her love and concern long prior to my boarding the train, and they called her "Granny" with evident affection.

The paper cups at the drinking fountain were exhausted, and the men were drinking water out of their cupped hands. "Granny" worried about this bacteria-laden practice until she remembered an old-fashioned collapsible drinking cup in her little zipper bag. She virtually turned the contents of the bag upside down before finding the cup; then she offered it to the soldiers radiantly. Thereafter, a steady stream of servicemen asked to borrow her cup. She yielded it up each time with gladness and words of smiling happiness.

During a pause in Richmond, the men sped to the station coffee shop, procured some pies, and came back onto the train without realizing that the pies had not been cut into sections. Since none of the men had a knife, one dashed to ask "Granny" if she had anything to cut pies with—as if a conventional lady in travel carried cutting weapons! She was not offended by the query but happy to turn her zipper bag again upside down until she found an orange stick. Apologetically, she passed the little stick on to the men with expressions of regret that she had nothing better suited to their purposes.

Later one of the soldiers sustained a mashed finger in playful attempt to keep a buddy out of the car. He rushed to "Granny" to ask if she had any first-aid materials. With considerable concern she foraged through her zipper bag until she found ointment and bandage. Then she bound up his finger with a generous portion of motherly advice concerning how to keep from getting an infection.

When there was a "cessation in hostilities" later, I asked of this aged and lovely lady, "Madam, you are a Christian, aren't you?"

"Yes," she replied. "I have been a Christian for more than seventy years. But why did you ask?"

"To tell the truth," I replied, "I wasn't asking for information. I was asking for confirmation of what I had felt to be true of you almost from the moment I sat alongside you. I just know that people do not come to be as completely and unselfishly concerned for the happiness of other people as I have observed you to be unless they have been with Jesus."

There are people who ride trains and buses with you and me. Or they work with us in our jobs, or spend much time with us in school activities, or live next door to us, or engage in sports and recreation with us. As they view our lives, do they take knowledge that we have been with Jesus? Let's face the important question again: Does my life in its daily walk give the proof supreme that I am a Christian?

Gracious Father, send every one of us from the period of examination with the resolution to bring every nook and corner of our lives into full harmony with the spirit and teachings of Jesus. May it be that all who walk with us in the days ahead, even the total stranger whom we touch in the way, will take knowledge of us, that we have been with Jesus. Amen.